Eight Questions of Faith

University of Nebraska Press

Lincoln

Eight Questions of Faith

Biblical Challenges That Guide and Ground Our Lives

NILES ELLIOT GOLDSTEIN

The Jewish Publication Society

Philadelphia

Library of Congress Cataloging-in-Publication Data
Goldstein, Niles Elliot, 1966– author.
Eight questions of faith: biblical challenges that guide
and ground our lives / Niles Elliot Goldstein.
    pages   cm
ISBN 978-0-8276-1219-8 (pbk.: alk. paper)
ISBN 978-0-8276-1242-6 (epub)
ISBN 978-0-8276-1243-3 (mobi)
ISBN 978-0-8276-1244-0 (pdf)
1. Faith (Judaism) 2. Bible. Old Testament—
Criticism, interpretation, etc. I. Title.
BM729.F3G65 2015   296.7—dc23   2015008906

Set in Arno Pro by L. Auten.

For my mother and father,
who gave me a safe haven
during a difficult time.
I will always be grateful for
your love and generosity.

Midway on our life's journey, I found myself
In dark woods, the right road lost. To tell
About those woods is hard—so tangled and rough

And savage that thinking of it now, I feel
The old fear stirring: death is hardly more bitter.

DANTE ALIGHIERI, *Inferno*

⌒

WIDE, the margin between carte blanche and the
white page. Nevertheless it is not in the margin
that you can find me, but in the yet whiter one that
separates the word-strewn sheet from the transparent,
the written page from the one to be written in the
infinite space where the eye turns back to the eye,
and the hand to the pen, where all we write is erased,
even as you write it. For the book imperceptibly
takes shape within the book we will never finish.

    There is my desert.

EDMUND JABÈS

⌒

Contents

Introduction

MIDWAY THROUGH MY LIFE, three pressing questions weighed down my soul.

First, there was the question of my marriage. I just didn't think I could do it anymore, it felt too dishonest. While I loved my wife, my heart told me that we weren't working as a couple, that our relationship needed to come to an end. Despite the truth I felt in my heart and my unwillingness or incapacity to fully commit to something I felt was wrong, my brain was torn by the issue: "Why should I leave a situation that had become so . . . familiar?" I drank alone at night in my basement cave to try to numb my uncertainty and doubts. If my situation didn't change, and soon, I would continue to damage my body and hide from the difficult reality that I was depressed.

Then there was the synagogue. Although I had been the spiritual leader of my Greenwich Village congregation since its founding, and while we'd weathered the horrors of 9/11, personal tragedies, and a catastrophic recession together—as well as celebrated births, marriages, and other joyous events—if I had to sit through another irritating board meeting or officiate at another idolatrous bar or bat mitzvah, I'd blow my brains out. After a decade of service, it was time for me to move on, and time for them find a new rabbi who wasn't disenchanted and burned out. But what should I do next?

Finally, after nearly twenty years of living and working there, I felt that I had reached the end of my relationship with New York City. The same frenetic energy that had fed me in my twenties and thirties was now devouring my soul. I'd come to loathe the city's unapologetic relentless-ness, its rat race sensibility, and its noise. By then, the noise enraged me most of all. Whether it was due to construction, a siren, or an incoming subway car, New York's oppressive din made it almost impossible for me to find peace. How could I remain in a city that was driving me to the end of my rope?

That summer, I left my wife, the synagogue, and New York, and I spent time by myself in a cabin near Hood River, Oregon.

Oregon wasn't an escape, it was a mirror—still, silent, and far removed from the frenzy of New York. I landed in Portland in early July, picked up my rental car, and drove east for an hour or so through the Columbia River Gorge until I emerged in the town of Hood River. Then, after stopping for supplies, I turned south toward Mount Hood and my isolated cabin that was tucked away in its foothills.

In my seclusion, I forced myself to face the life-altering choices that loomed before me. Within two months, I'd be unemployed for the first time in my life. I asked myself, *What am I going to do next, a rabbi who has no desire to serve another congregation?* And then I turned to the more emotional and frightening question: *Should I get a divorce from a woman I still care about?* These two questions reverberated inside my soul day and night, whether I was on a hike, river rafting, going for a drive, or watching the sunset. I couldn't shake them—and I wouldn't let myself. Was I about to enter a brave new world and free myself from the burdens of boredom and despair, or was I, like Ahab, a wounded man in midlife pursuing a "phantom" that would either elude me or drive me to the ends of the earth—and, perhaps, self-destruction?

All I had were questions.

I found solace at a brewpub in nearby Parkdale. On many evenings, I would sit on the back deck, drink beer, pet the dogs that roamed the grounds, and watch the sun gradually sink behind Mount Hood. Those were the only moments when I had contact with other human beings, and I became friendly with a local woman who had grown up in the area. She was newly divorced herself, and we spoke about her own doubts and fears prior to making the decision to end her marriage, about the challenges of throwing in the towel and starting again from scratch.

The woman's parents lived about half an hour east on a small farm on the outskirts of The Dalles, and they were horse trainers by trade. She invited me to join her on a sunset ride one afternoon, and I readily accepted. When I arrived at the farm, her father, grizzled but polite, was already saddling up the horses. Her mother asked me questions about living in New York and confessed that she had never traveled outside of Oregon. Their marriage seemed warm and solid; they'd been partners, both personally and professionally, for a very long time. It made me think about how my own marriage was on its last legs. As we rode our horses over brown hills and brush, and as deer and pheasants darted out of our path, I wondered why a comfortable partnership wasn't enough for me. What was I seeking with such restlessness, and why?

Yet again, all I had were questions.

After almost two weeks away, I'd resolved nothing about the decisions that awaited me back home but that I knew could no longer be pushed aside. What were my options? I could brood alone in the cabin, numb myself with booze, or get outside and at least feel like I was part of a larger reality beyond my inner turmoil. On the morning before my return flight, I drove over the Bridge of the Gods, crossed the border into Washington, and entered Gifford Pinchot National Forest, a wilderness area in the heart of the volcanic Cascade mountain range. I decided to hike up Sawtooth Trail, a former section of the famous Pacific Crest Trail that stretches from Mexico to Canada.

The arduous trail climbed up to the fifty-four-hundred-foot summit in virtually a straight shot, and I was dripping with sweat ninety minutes later when I finally broke through the tree line and reached the exposed but level ridge at the top of Sawtooth Mountain. The setting was spectacular. Wind howled over the summit; craggy boulders crammed the peak; any misstep would lead to a sheer fall of thousands of feet. From that uneasy perch, there was a 360-degree view of Mount St. Helens to the west, Mount Rainier to the north, and Mount Hood to the south. While I couldn't actually make it out, I sensed the Pacific Ocean as its waves muscled inexorably into the rugged coastline on one side of me; on the other, great rolling plains unraveled east as far as my eyes could see. I was just a speck, a bag of bones surrounded by an unfathomable enormity.

I began to cry. I'd never felt so starkly alive, yet so profoundly lost, at the same time. "What am I supposed to do?" I asked aloud. "What happens now?"

The reply to my query was silence. That was the gospel of the mountain.

At this stage of my life, would I have the maturity and strength to tolerate that kind of ambiguity? It was too early to tell. I looked for an answer through the lens of my faith tradition. The gospel of Sawtooth was, for me, the gospel of Sinai—mystery, ineffability, at times even silence. While Moses received the Torah from God on top of the desert mountain, its many laws and teachings often raise more questions than they answer: What is the meaning of life? Why do I exist? Where am I heading?

It is questions such as these that have preoccupied my mind (and transformed my life) in recent years, both as a rabbi and as a man.

I have written this book, in part, to share my search. And because I know I am not the only one who voices these queries.

What has intrigued me most about the Hebrew Bible specifically is not its dramatic stories, colorful characters, or moral lessons, but its *questions*. These many and varied questions are profound, pedagogic, rhetorical, challenging, at times even painful. Some of them are famous and some infamous; some have elevated souls and others have humbled them. Many of these questions are voiced by biblical figures, while others are attributed to God, either through intermediaries or directly. At their core, almost all of these questions are as relevant and compelling today as they were in antiquity.

This book explores the following questions:

~ How do we live when we know we are going to die?
~ Why is humility so important?
~ Are we responsible for other people?
~ What is the purpose of human life?
~ Is some knowledge too dangerous to possess?
~ Has God abandoned us?
~ How do we return when we have lost our way?
~ What happens to us after we die?

These are questions that all of us ask at one time or another, in varying order, during the course of our lives. As I have strived to navigate through the transitions of midlife—and my own personal and spiritual trials— these inquiries have granted me a paradoxical sense of security, an invisible yet very palpable feeling of comfort and community. They've shown me that, in all my perplexity, I am far from alone.

The Bible is neither a philosophical treatise nor, in my view, a roadmap for redemption. It is instead a complex, existential expression of uncertainty and confusion, of yearning and hope, of wonderment, suffering, and joy. The Bible, and the timeless questions interwoven in it, is a testament to, and a portrait of, the valleys and peaks of the human condition. It doesn't offer us rigid answers; it graces us with fellowship.

This book highlights several of the signposts of the human journey— and offers, I hope, a framework through which we can find more guidance for and meaning in our own lives. *Eight Questions of Faith* takes us into the psycho-spiritual muck and mire of concepts such as mortality, sin, responsibility, fear, courage, and the afterlife, drawing not only from the rabbinic and mystical traditions but also from insights in philosophy, psychology, literature, and real experience.

What you hold in your hands is not a linear, verse-by-verse commentary or a systematic examination of the Bible's "greatest hits" of human inquiry. It is a very personal book constructed around questions that I myself have asked—using different words and in different contexts—in my life, questions I have also encountered, repeatedly, from others whom I have counseled or conversed with over my nearly two decades in the rabbinate. They have regularly served as springboards for intense and passionate conversations, often with life-altering consequences.

The conversations have not been easy.

In the *Divine Comedy*, Dante finds enlightenment only after, having become disoriented, he enters a dark forest. Similarly, the skin on the face of Moses becomes "radiant" only after he enters the thick, smoky cloud that covers Mount Sinai at the moment of divine revelation. The message seems clear: it is in the heart of unknowing, the "thick darkness" where the *lack* of clarity fuels a hunger for answers, that we mature, evolve, and ultimately discover our true path. Viewed in this way, perplexity is as much a gift as it is a source of discomfort, a conduit toward inner advancement as well as a crucible through which our minds and souls are pushed to their breaking points.

I wrote this book for anyone who questions or quests, seeks or sojourns. May it—and the ageless questions it explores—grant solace to the restless and fellowship to the forlorn. May it bring us closer to truth, to each other, and ultimately to our God.

Eight Questions of Faith

1

Between Cradle and Grave

~

THE SUMMER AFTER MY TRIP to Oregon, my wife and I decided to get a divorce. While we looked like a good couple on paper—we both loved to travel, we came from similar educational and Jewish backgrounds, we shared a quirky sense of humor—we weren't making each other happy. And frankly, I wasn't ready for the commitment and discipline of marriage. I had talked myself into our union, seeking counsel from my friends, family, and therapist, but I was never really present for my wife in the way that she deserved. I felt guilty for that, inadequate, and ashamed.

Several months before, I'd parted ways with the congregation I'd helped to found. Major differences had emerged between my vision for the shul and that of our lay leadership. While I fought for more robust (and overt) religiosity in our services and programs, my board favored the social dimension; its focus on food and fun was, in my view, dwarfing talk of ritual and God. I also had to contend with creative but strong-willed founders who wouldn't let go and cede power to others. Taken together, these new realities made my experience as a spiritual leader intolerable.

I also moved out of New York. Now that my marriage and my longtime job had both come to an end, there was nothing to keep me there any longer—and I was sick of the city anyway. I'd avoided getting sucked into the narcissism of New York, a mind-set that made the rest of the country seem like a suburb. As an author and teacher, I'd spoken in other cities all over the country, and I knew firsthand that there were plenty of happy people who lived outside the Big Apple. I'd actually come to envy their much better quality of life and the far more human pace by which they lived.

These changes were important and necessary. Yet having them all occur at the same time—that was surreal. And soon they came to feel overwhelming.

One year after I made the biggest decisions of my life, I stood high above the jagged shoreline of Lake Superior. I'd been invited by a synagogue to lead a retreat in Michigan's Upper Peninsula, and I stayed on afterward to do some traveling and hiking on my own. It was early fall, and it had been over two decades since I last set foot in the UP. I viewed my journey there as a pilgrimage of sorts, a return to a place that had given me a measure of solace at another time of transition, following college graduation. So much had occurred during the intervening years. Maybe too much.

My life was still unsettled, personally and professionally. I had moved back to Chicago, where I grew up, but I was living as an adult in my parents' condo downtown; all of my books and other meaningful possessions were in storage in Yonkers. I hadn't yet landed a new full-time position, and I wasn't even sure what it was that I wanted to do with the next chapter of my life. I had failed at marriage and I continued to struggle with commitment. Mainly to distract myself from my feelings of pain and humiliation, I was drinking and debauching like a teenager. But this state of limbo was taking its toll on me. I didn't know how much more uncertainty and anxiety I could endure. There were days when, for no apparent reason, I'd suddenly burst into tears.

A few days after the retreat, I drove to the trailhead of one of the UP's most spectacular hikes, the Chapel Loop, a twelve-mile trail that cuts through the center and outer edges of Pictured Rocks National Lakeshore. On the loop trail, I passed birch, beech, and pine trees, streams, waterfalls, and small lakes. After a few miles, the trail opened onto the southern shore of Lake Superior, where I saw Chapel Rock itself. Like the other rock formations along the lakeshore, Chapel Rock was sculpted by erosion from the wind, ice, and waves. As the trail climbed steeply, I looked down from sheer sandstone cliffs and saw arches, turrets, and dunes. The sky was gray and the wind was strong. Whitecaps rolled toward the shore and crashed into coves and caves below me.

Not long afterward, I reached a particularly stunning and exposed ridge just off the trail. I walked to the very edge and gazed down at the churning water. Chapel Rock was no longer in sight, but its symbolism was not lost on me. As I stood alone, buffeted by wind, my life adrift, there was no sanctuary left to protect me. Here I was, in the middle of life's journey, confronted by what seemed like endless bewilderment and sorrow. I was an outsider, someone unable to fit into a stable, normal path. It felt harder to hold myself back than to leap into Lake Superior. *Why go on?* I asked myself. It would be so easy to jump, to kiss the void rather than to get back on the trail and continue my journey into the dark forest. Death might be a mystery, but so was life. What was the difference? My heart raced. Adrenaline coursed through my body. The impulse to end things felt irresistible—and it scared the hell out of me.

The seconds seemed like an eternity. Yet with genuine effort, and with utter terror at the power and pull of my temptation, I backed away from the edge.

I chose life. But I could have just as easily made the other decision.

What most likely drew me away from the cliff was less the result of rational, conscious deliberation than of intuition, a gut feeling that my mission on the earth as a man and as a rabbi was not yet over. I wasn't ready to die and I had much more to give. As difficult as life seemed at the moment, I held on to the hope that the place in which I stood—a place of anxiety, despair, and frustration—would end. I felt overwhelmed by my past decisions and angry about my current state of uncertainty. I was also world-weary and haunted by great doubts about ever being able to fit in. Yet my challenges could have been worse. I had a roof over my head and parents to lean on. Like so many others who had struggled and suffered before me, I'd somehow get back on my feet.

I had to. If I didn't believe in myself, nobody else would.

"Why did I ever issue from the womb?" (Jeremiah 20:18)

This first inquiry is as relevant as it is ancient. How many of us, when we have gone through agonizing and dark episodes in our own lives, have asked ourselves this question? It may not be universal, but it is certainly commonplace. As I know from my own and others' experiences, when relationships and marriages fall apart, when confusion grips our minds, when unemployment seems like a snare from which we can't break free, when addictions crush our bodies and spirits, it is a very rare sort of human being who does *not* wish, even momentarily, for everything to come to an end.

Death is an appealing prospect when life's trials feel insurmountable.

In this particular case, the question is asked by the prophet Jeremiah. "Why did I ever issue from the womb?" (Jer. 20:18) occurs within the larger context of what are known as Jeremiah's "confessions," emotionally rich and deeply personal passages that have no real parallel in the Hebrew Bible's other books. Jeremiah speaks here in his own name; the "I" he refers to in these passages is not God, as in the biblical book's other oracular sections, but himself. The only other book that even remotely comes close to this style and tone is Lamentations, the masterwork of biblical gloom and doom—a text that is, not coincidentally, attributed by the classical tradition to the prophet Jeremiah himself.

AN OUTBURST OF PAIN AND DESPAIR

The life of Jeremiah (645–580 BCE) spanned a critical period in the history of Judah, the southern part of what had become, as a result of civil war, a divided Israelite kingdom. Other than a brief period of independence, Judah had devolved from a regional power into a vassal state and a political pawn under the successive and oppressive empires of Assyria, Egypt, and Babylonia. The northern kingdom of Israel had ceased to exist—it had fallen to the Assyrians a century before Jeremiah was even born. A weak, wounded Judah was all that was left of a once strong, unified Jewish nation. But it, too, was coming to a violent end. Jeremiah would bear witness to its horrific destruction and travel with his people into exile. He would be the monarchy's last prophet.

Like other biblical prophets (such as Moses and Jonah), Jeremiah at first resists his call to divine service. In the very first chapter of the book, we see his protest:

Ah, Lord GOD!
I don't know how to speak,
For I am still a boy. (Jer. 1:6)

But God tells Jeremiah not to be afraid, not to recoil from his mission no matter how daunting it may seem. God promises to be with him during the difficult days ahead. Jeremiah is forewarned of a disaster that will strike from the north, yet he does not know at the outset of his prophetic journey that the cataclysm will take concrete form in the siege of Israel by Babylonia. Jeremiah's sacred mandate is to sound the alarm among his people and urge them to repent of their moral and spiritual transgressions before it is too late.

The prophet carries out his mission. Jeremiah publicly warns the Israelites of the impending calamity, the invasion that God is directing—using Babylonian troops as God's agents—as punishment for their crimes. But he also experiences, and expresses verbally, the pain and loneliness he feels as the sole harbinger of such great ruination:

> Oh, my suffering, my suffering!
> How I writhe!
> Oh, the walls of my heart!
> My heart moans within me,
> I cannot be silent. . . .
> Suddenly my tents have been ravaged,
> In a moment, my tent cloths.
> How long must I see standards
> And hear the blare of horns? (Jer. 4:19–21)

It isn't clear whether Jeremiah is describing a present event or having a premonition of a future one. What is clear is the agony his prophetic detachment causes in him.

While Jeremiah accepts his role, he is ambivalent about his people. On the one hand, he grieves for his fellow countrymen:

> When in grief I would seek comfort,
> My heart is sick within me. . . .
> Because my people is shattered I am shattered;
> I am dejected, seized by desolation.
> Is there no balm in Gilead? (Jer. 8:18, 21–22)

On the other hand, he recoils from them in disgust:

> Oh, to be in the desert,
> At an encampment for wayfarers!
> Oh, to leave my people,
> To go away from them—
> For they are all adulterers,
> A band of rogues. (Jer. 9:1)

Jeremiah has no option but to play the part his destiny demands. God chose him and in so doing set him apart from the rest of his people; that choice sentenced him, in effect, to a life of isolation and torment:

> You enticed me, o Lord, and I was enticed;
> You overpowered me and You prevailed.
> I have become a constant laughingstock,
> Everyone jeers at me....
> For the word of the Lord causes me
> Constant disgrace and contempt. (Jer. 20:7–8)

Jeremiah heeds his call to duty, but it too is rooted in ambivalence and conflict. Whenever Jeremiah attempts to throw off the burden of his prophetic mantle, he finds that he just can't do it:

> I thought, "I will not mention Him,
> No more will I speak in His name"—
> But [His word] was like a raging fire in my heart,
> Shut up in my bones;
> I could not hold it in, I was helpless. (Jer. 20:9)

Though he craves escape from the painful scorn his role has brought him, Jeremiah confesses that he is unable to hold himself back from speaking the word of God. Since the book begins with a description of God placing divine words into Jeremiah's mouth, this doesn't come as a complete surprise. Jeremiah has become a conduit for God's message, and he now fully grasps the terrible existential consequences of that transformation:

I have not sat in the company of revelers
And made merry!
I have sat lonely because of Your hand upon me,
For You have filled me with gloom.
Why must my pain be endless,
My wound incurable,
Resistant to healing? (Jer. 15:17–18)

Jeremiah's question may very well be rhetorical, a verbal expression of his inner angst, perhaps even anger. Yet it is his next question that is truly revealing, for it discloses that Jeremiah has reached the point of suicidal despair. In a raw outburst of emotion, of suffering, regret, anguish, and rage, he cries out:

Accursed be the day
That I was born!
Let not the day be blessed
When my mother bore me!
Accursed be the man
Who brought my father the news
And said, "A boy
Is born to you,"
And gave him such joy! . . .
Because he did not kill me before birth
So that my mother might be my grave. . . .
Why did I ever issue from the womb,
To see misery and woe,
To spend all my days in shame? (Jer. 20:14–15, 17–18)

These are the tortured words of a man in a state of existential crisis, someone who wishes he had never entered the world at all. In the biblical and religious context, his words—which amount to a spiteful rejection of an act of God's love, the gift of life—seem blasphemous. Yet Jeremiah's question lays bare a death wish, a desire to escape from a life that has become unbearable for him. The personal loneliness and public derision that have accompanied his prophetic office are too much for him. Why did he have to be born, he implies, if life was going to be so wretched and painful?

Death would be a welcome alternative.

It is the experience of loss, and of being lost, that often triggers this kind of yearning. Yet where is the boundary between wanting to die and wishing that you'd never left the womb? Do these impulses represent two discrete desires, or do they express the same longing, but in different ways?

In *The Balcony*, the French playwright Jean Genet (1910–86) refers to the human journey as "a quest for immobility." What does he mean? I think Genet is saying that all of us, deep down and perhaps even unconsciously, hunger for a halt to our seemingly ceaseless moving, roving, and being. We crave rest and peace. We yearn to cast away our burdens and, as Shakespeare put it in *Hamlet*, to "shuffle off this mortal coil." In this sense, immobility—whether represented by a corpse in the earth or, to use Jeremiah's image, a fetus in the womb—is a source of liberation, of stillness, silence, and serenity.

Jeremiah's question cuts straight to the heart of the human condition. Through his rhetorical outburst, the prophet expresses much of the pain, frustration, anger, grief, loneliness, and yearning that so many of us have felt at different times and in different places, from antiquity to the present. Which leads inevitably to the great paradox: embedded in the experience of living our lives is the longing to be freed from the tumult and tribulation of life itself.

Other biblical figures verbalize similar world-weary (and often self-destructive) feelings and desires. At times, these expressions take the form of questions. In the book of Ecclesiastes, after the jaded king famously proclaims, "Utter futility! All is futile!" (Eccles. 1:2), he then asks himself a basic question that evolves into a monologue:

What real value is there for a man
In all the gains he makes beneath the sun?
One generation goes, another comes,
But the earth remains the same forever.
The sun rises, and the sun sets—
And glides back to where it rises.
Southward blowing,
Turning northward,
Ever turning blows the wind;
On its rounds the wind returns.
All streams flow into the sea,
Yet the sea is never full;
To the place [from] which they flow
The streams flow back again.
All such things are wearisome:
No man can ever state them;
The eye never has enough of seeing,
Nor the ear enough of hearing.
Only that shall happen
Which has happened,
Only that occur
Which has occurred;
There is nothing new
Beneath the sun!

Sometimes there is a phenomenon of which they say, "Look, this one is new!"—it occurred long since, in ages that went by before us. The earlier ones are not remembered; so too those that will occur later will no more be remembered than those that will occur at the very end. (Eccles. 1:3–11)

What begins as a question about the benefits of our labor quickly becomes—refracted through the lens of the king's reflective mind—a meditation on time. For Kohelet, the man speaking in Ecclesiastes, human toil is an exercise in futility and pointlessness. Anything we do has been done before; all that is created will perish and then be re-created. Memory will preserve nothing. Even the cycles of the natural world are exercises in repetition. Heraclitus, the ancient Greek philosopher, argued that no one could step into the same river twice. Kohelet claims exactly the opposite. In his view, existence is *not* in a state of perpetual change and transformation; it is, instead, forever bound by the laws of stasis.

While Jeremiah (a prophet called individually by God) focuses on his own unique struggle and pain, Kohelet (a man who inherits the dynastic crown) draws from his personal journey but then, in a more philosophical and abstract way, makes an assessment about human life in general. In the end, it isn't a very uplifting one.

Kohelet the king first addresses the topic of pleasure. What is the purpose of life? When we are children and in our youth, the pursuit of pleasure is often the driving force behind many of our actions. As we mature, those things that give us pleasure usually evolve along with us—we crave wealth, knowledge, success, renown. Nonetheless, it is the same pursuit of pleasure that motivates us.

The king challenges himself: "I said to myself, 'Come, I will treat you to merriment. Taste mirth!' . . . What good is that?" (Eccles. 2:1–2).

Kohelet then answers his own question by sharing his personal experiences:

I ventured to tempt my flesh with wine, and to grasp folly, while letting my mind direct with wisdom, to the end that I might learn which of the two was better for men to practice in their few days of life under heaven. I multiplied my possessions. I built myself houses and I planted vineyards. I laid out gardens and groves, in which I planted every kind of fruit tree. I constructed pools of water, enough to irrigate a forest shooting up with trees. I bought male and female slaves, and I acquired stewards. I also acquired more cattle, both herds and flocks, than all who were before me in Jerusalem. I further amassed silver and gold and treasures of kings and provinces; and I got myself male and female singers, as well as the luxuries of commoners—coffers and coffers of them. Thus, I gained more wealth than anyone before me in Jerusalem. In addition, my wisdom remained with me: I withheld from my eyes nothing they asked for, and denied myself no enjoyment; rather, I got enjoyment out of all my wealth. And that was all I got out of my wealth. (Eccles. 2:3–10)

In an attempt to uncover the true purpose of human life, the king tries to satiate himself with carnal delights, with wine, women, and song. He accumulates riches, homes, and lands; he owns massive herds; he controls legions of slaves (all marks of affluence for a sovereign of his era). Kohelet is concerned with his legacy as well. He constructs great public works, reservoirs and aqueducts, gardens and parks. He experiences, possesses, and achieves beyond the imaginings of most mortals.

Yet he is, in the end, still mortal. Despite everything the king has gained and accomplished, he concludes that the pursuit of pleasure that drove his actions is ultimately purposeless and pointless. Like Jeremiah, Kohelet offers another saturnine, though arguably less angry, expression of despair and futility: "Then my thoughts turned to all the fortune my hands had built up, to the wealth I had acquired and won—and oh, it was all futile and pursuit of wind; there was no real value under the sun!" (Eccles. 2:11).

Having dismissed pleasure as a successful pathway to "the good," Kohelet turns next to a different kind of pursuit, the pursuit of wisdom:

My thoughts also turned to appraising wisdom and madness and folly. I found that

Wisdom is superior to folly
As light is superior to darkness;
A wise man has his eyes in his head,
Whereas a fool walks in darkness.

But I also realized that the same fate awaits them both. So I reflected: "The fate of the fool is also destined for me; to what advantage, then, have I been wise?" And I came to the conclusion that that too was futile, because the wise man, just like the fool, is not remembered forever; for, as the succeeding days roll by, both are forgotten. Alas, the wise man dies, just like the fool! (Eccles. 2:12–16)

While there are some short-term temporal benefits to wisdom, the end for both the sage and the fool is the same: death is the great equalizer. As a result, Kohelet concludes, the pursuit of wisdom is meaningless as well, an act of utter futility.

To be human is to strive and to toil, yet Kohelet argues that both activities are nothing more than the "pursuit of wind." If rich and poor, sage and fool, all suffer the same fate, what is the point of anything at all? The implication of the king's observations mirrors that of Jeremiah's question, *Why were we ever born?* This brings Kohelet to a very dark place, where he conveys, if not an overt death wish, then at least a profound regret about existence itself: "And so I loathed life. For I was distressed by all that goes on under the sun, because everything is futile and pursuit of wind" (Eccles. 2:17).

Kohelet may be more philosophical, and Jeremiah more emotional, in their verbal expressions about mortality and mission, but their underlying question is essentially the same: When all is said and done, is human life really worth it?

Jeremiah pleads for the cessation of his pain. Kohelet strives to find meaning in his labor. And though the two men lived centuries apart, both of them are highly concerned (either implicitly or explicitly) with memory, with being remembered, respected, and relevant, even after they have died.

Most scholars think that the book of Ecclesiastes was written during the Hellenistic period in Palestine, in the third or fourth century BCE, and the author clearly displays ample evidence of being influenced by Greek Stoicism. A few centuries later, the Stoic philosopher and Roman emperor Marcus Aurelius (121–180 CE) would write in his *Meditations* that "the memory of everything is very soon overwhelmed in time."

Kings will eventually be forgotten. Monuments will crumble and vanish. Sages, heroes, palaces, herds—nothing will leave a lasting memory in the eternity of the cosmos. In this respect, Kohelet and Marcus Aurelius are just two of the countless thinkers and writers who have mused on the link between mortality and memory.

What happens when we let our vanity get in the way, when our acts of hubris crash into the inescapably transitory nature of existence? In "Ozymandias," the English poet Percy Bysshe Shelley (1792–1822) uses verse to create a compelling image of the outcome:

I met a traveller from an antique land
Who said: "Two vast and trunkless legs of stone
Stand in the desert. Near them, on the sand,
Half sunk, a shattered visage lies, whose frown,
And wrinkled lip, and sneer of cold command,
Tell that its sculptor well those passions read
Which yet survive, stamped on these lifeless things,
The hand that mocked them and the heart that fed.
And on the pedestal these words appear—
'My name is Ozymandias, king of kings:
Look on my works, ye Mighty, and despair!'
Nothing beside remains. Round the decay
Of that colossal wreck, boundless and bare
The lone and level sands stretch far away."

Shelley's poem is more than a famous expression of nineteenth-century Romanticism; it is a statement about finitude and the human condition, a cautionary tale for all those who seek to be remembered or, to use Kohelet's language, who strive after the wind. In the Jewish liturgy, the following words are recited aloud during the prayer known as the *Aleinu*: "We bow down in worship and praise before the king of king of kings, the Holy One, blessed be He." Some scholars interpret these words as a veiled polemic against the conventional appellation ("king of kings") bestowed on ancient rulers such as Ozymandias. In Jewish theology, the only sovereign who transcends time and space is God. Temporal power is and will forever be precisely that—temporary.

Yet if even the memory of mighty kings will disintegrate and blow away with the sands, then what will become of us? How do we not succumb to despair?

As we see through the words of Jeremiah and Kohelet, when we reach an awareness of our own transience and fragility, it is only natural to feel powerful emotions, especially those of anger and sorrow. Yet that same consciousness can serve as a catalyst for growth, an opportunity to uncover within ourselves capacities for courage and fortitude we never knew we possessed.

Our challenge is to live our lives as fully and deeply as we can, even in the face of our impermanence and, from the perspective of some, our ultimate irrelevance.

A MATTER OF INTELLECTUAL INQUIRY

It seems clear that the questions posed by both Jeremiah and Kohelet are largely rhetorical, more expressions of emotion (and pathos) than a genuine desire to probe for potential answers. Yet others, while addressing the same source of perplexity and vexation, have attempted to move past emotionality and toward a better intellectual understanding of Jeremiah's anguished query, "Why did I ever issue from the womb?"

Franz Rosenzweig (1886–1929) was an important modern Jewish thinker and a German veteran of the First World War. While stationed at the front, he wrote thousands of words onto military postcards that he then mailed home. Eventually, many of these observations and ideas became the foundation of his masterwork, *The Star of Redemption*. The opening sentence of that book has always resonated with me in deep and personal ways, from the time I first read it in rabbinical school to the present day, when ruminations and concerns about life and death have become signature experiences in my own midlife journey. Rosenzweig starts his book with the following line: "From death, it is from the fear of death that all cognition of the All begins."

In Rosenzweig's worldview, we cannot run away from the reality of death, nor escape the fear that it inevitably engenders in us all. Instead, he argues for an honest acknowledgment and bold acceptance of this existential fact. We find no outburst of rage or expression of grief in Rosenzweig's words. He is someone who has witnessed death firsthand, and he likely knows on a raw, primal level that it is an unavoidable part of human existence. In actuality, our fear of death is what makes us human, what makes us self-aware. The French philosopher René Descartes (1596–1650) may have famously written, "I think, therefore I am" (in *Discourse on the Method*), but Rosenzweig offers a different approach: *I die, therefore I am.*

We cannot possibly attempt to fathom the "All," the enormity and totality of existence, unless and until we grasp the reality of the individual.

Rosenzweig was in large measure rebelling against German Idealism, a philosophical movement that emerged in the late eighteenth and early nineteenth centuries. One of the central tenets of Idealism was that "things-in-themselves" (separate from and independent of our perception or experience of them) did not truly exist. For Rosenzweig, this is lunacy; death is a reality independent of human minds, and our response to that reality—fear—is neither misguided nor delusional. He writes in *The Star of Redemption,*

> All that is mortal lives in this fear of death; every new birth multiplies the fear for a new reason, for it multiplies that which is mortal. The womb of the inexhaustible earth ceaselessly gives birth to what is new, and each one is subject to death; each newly born waits with fear and trembling for the day of passage into the dark.

To be human is to be mortal, and to be mortal is to die. The resulting fear that inheres in human existence is natural and inescapable. It is also unique for every person. As Rosenzweig continues in *The Star*, each experience of fear renews our sense of being alive:

> Man does not want to escape from some chain [of being]; he wants to stay, he wants—to live.... The fear of the earthly should be removed from him only with the earthly itself. But as long as he lives on earth, he should also remain in fear of the earthly.... In fact, all cognition of the All has for its presupposition—nothing. For the one and universal cognition of the All, only the one and universal nothing is valid.... The nothing of death is a something, each renewed nothing of death is a renewed something that frightens anew, and that cannot be passed over in silence, nor be silenced.... If death is something, then no philosophy is again going to make us avert our eyes with its assertion that it presupposes nothing.

Our existential terror results from the very real fact of our mortality; it is not a response to a myth or a lie. Since Idealism elevates knowledge of the All over awareness of the one, it totalizes (and thus destroys) our singularity as individual human beings. Rosenzweig preserves our particularity by viewing death in a "positive" way. The fact that death is real, and that each one of us fears it, demonstrates in and of itself that we, too, are real. As unique, self-aware beings, we are also *relevant*. Rather than vanishing into the vastness of the cosmic totality, we stand within it—frightened, perhaps lonely, but alive, identifiable, and necessary. For Rosenzweig, that is significance enough.

While *The Star of Redemption* begins with the words "from death," the book concludes with the words "into life." The bonds between death and life, fear and self-awareness, mortality and affirmation are profound in Rosenzweig's metaphysical system. Like the intersecting lines of the star of redemption itself (a diagram that is identical to the two triangles that constitute the star of David), everything is interrelated and interconnected. After careful inquiry, Rosenzweig posits hope, not outrage and despair, as the appropriate response to the human condition. Although our bodies may decay and our names be forgotten, each of us who has entered the world contributes to the harmony of the All, and every one of us—in our own individuality—possesses unique worth. It is through this singular value that our lives, and the world, will ultimately be redeemed.

Nearly a millennium before Rosenzweig was born, another Jewish thinker explored the relationship between death and life—and the challenge of how to transcend the tendency to slip into a mood of gloom and doom when we ponder our mortality. Rabbi Moses Maimonides (1135–1204) was a philosopher, writer, and physician, and he is widely acknowledged as one of the greatest theologians of the medieval era; his influence on Jewish thought continues to this day. A prolific author, Maimonides wrote books both for the general public and for the scholarly elite. *The Guide for the Perplexed* is his philosophical magnum opus, and the book's final chapter addresses how the reality of death can affect the nature and quality of our life.

Maimonides explains this often-vexing dynamic in a way that is more uplifting than the emotional expressions of Jeremiah and Kohelet and more inspirational than even the hopefulness offered by Rosenzweig. In the *Guide*, Maimonides describes how (for some) an existential awareness of death can become the catalyst for ecstatic experience, a sort of philosophical and psychic euphoria that arrives just as life begins to slip away:

> When an enlightened man is stricken with years and approaches death, this apprehension [of the intellectual love of God] increases very powerfully, joy over this apprehension and a great love for the object of apprehension become stronger, until the soul is separated from the body at that moment in this state of pleasure. Because of this the Sages have indicated with reference to the deaths of Moses, Aaron, and Miriam that "the three of them died by a kiss." ... Their purpose was to indicate that the three of them died in the pleasure of this apprehension due to the intensity of passionate love.

As a Scholastic thinker who was influenced by Aristotle, Maimonides's idea of the summum bonum, or highest good, was the life of the mind, the pursuit of knowledge through reason. As a rabbi and a theist, however, he believed that knowledge had to be focused on a particular object: God. In this context, the knowledge of God and "enlightenment" are identical, and the love that emerges when one's intellect reaches its most profound goal is a natural consequence. For such a person, the approach of death only intensifies his or her experience of joy and love, since death is the gateway that frees the mind from the limitations and constraints of bodily existence. The enlightened soul craves *olam ha-ba*, the world-to-come, an eternal, euphoric state of intellectual interconnection with God.

In a certain respect, Maimonides describes a philosophical version of the same passionate yearning expressed by Jeremiah, Kohelet, and so many others—the desire to free ourselves of those features of mortal life that challenge us, impede us, and pain us.

Why does Maimonides single out Moses, Aaron, and Miriam as paradigms for enlightened human beings? The Torah informs us that the three of them were siblings, and it is clear from the text that they were also the primary leaders of the Israelites at a pivotal time in Jewish history: during the exodus from Egypt, the revelation at Mount Sinai, and the forty years of wandering in the desert. Further, Moses, Aaron, and Miriam all die before their people reach the Promised Land. For Maimonides (in keeping with the midrashic legend about God's "kiss of death"), this is not a tragedy. While they fail to enter the physical space of the Holy Land, they gain something far more important—a *meta*physical vision, a passionate, loving, and intellectual apprehension of the Holy One. He writes in the *Guide*,

> In this dictum the Sages, may their memory be blessed, followed the generally accepted poetical way of expression that calls the apprehension that is achieved in a state of intense and passionate love for Him, may He be exalted, "a kiss," in accordance with its dictum: "Let him kiss me with the kisses of his mouth . . ." (Song of Songs 1:2) The Sages, may their memory be blessed, mention the occurrence of this kind of death, which in true reality is salvation from death, only with regard to "Moses, Aaron, and Miriam."

Modern scholars have noted that the kiss of God is often used in midrashic and mystical literature as a metaphor for union with the divine, a kiss that does not bring about death, but the *death* of death. Moses, Aaron, and Miriam do not really "die"; while their bodies ultimately disappear, they themselves live on in an eternal state of ecstatic communion—a reward for their fidelity, leadership, and intimate knowledge of God.

Yet what of the rest of us? Is "salvation from death" not possible for ordinary human beings? In what appears to be a departure from the view of his rabbinic forbears, Maimonides writes that if we achieve philosophical wisdom, awareness of death can intensify our capacity for intellectual love of God and help us to realize a permanent state of mystical ecstasy, "the impediment that sometimes screened [them] off having been removed." The end of life can lead to more focused thought, a focus that can help us to shed the everyday distractions, concerns, and ego-needs that prevent us from a true clarity of vision—from enlightenment. In this sense, every human being has the inner potential to become like Moses, Aaron, and Miriam, to experience the death of death.

Why did we come out of the womb? Why were we ever born, if none of us can avoid fear, pain, toil, and our own inevitable demise? Some thinkers provide answers that offer hope, that help to lift our spirits when we feel wounded or broken. For Rosenzweig, it is in order to participate in the harmony of the All, to assume our unique position in the cosmic totality. For Maimonides, it is to strive for philosophical wisdom, to attain an intellectual love of God that has the power to "save" us from physical death.

Writers and artists have expressed Jeremiah's question in many and varied ways as well, sometimes indirectly. Ernest Hemingway (1899–1961), in his novel *The Old Man and the Sea*, writes of the thrashing but ultimately doomed marlin on the end of Santiago's line: "He is much fish still and I saw that the hook was in the corner of his mouth and he has kept his mouth tight shut. The punishment of the hook is nothing. The punishment of hunger, and that he is against something he does not comprehend, is everything."

Many of us can tolerate pain and suffering, especially if we know that the experience will eventually pass or that it has something to teach us from which we will grow. Misery without end or purpose, however, can feel intolerable. Hemingway's marlin is strong, and it is not deeply troubled by the sting of the hook. What *is* torturous to the fish is that, while it struggles and starves, it cannot grasp the reason. The difference between animals and human beings is that our discomfort and anguish—particularly in the face of an inescapable mortality that we were never given a choice about—often motivate us to inquire into a situation that seems completely unfathomable.

Our questions are the outer signs of our own hunger: the craving for meaning.

Like many other artists, Paul Gauguin (1848–1903) was interested in life's great—and frequently inscrutable—questions. One of his masterpieces is a very large, enigmatic depiction of a kind of Polynesian Eden, filled with archetypal figures in various states and stages of life. It is entitled *Where Do We Come From? What Are We? Where Are We Going?* The work was painted, according to the artist, before he attempted suicide in 1897. Through his personal actions, Gauguin seems to suggest a clear link between the perplexing nature of human existence and the often-seductive pull of nihilistic despair.

If we can steel ourselves against the temptations of nihilism, however, our craving for meaning can create an invaluable opportunity for transformation and advancement.

We find a strikingly similar antecedent to Gauguin's tripartite title in one of the classic texts of rabbinic literature, *Pirke Avot* (The sayings of the fathers). The following series of questions is attributed to the mishnaic sage Akavia ben Mahalalel: "Where have you come from? Where are you going? Before whom will you have to give an accounting?" (*Avot* 3:1). The answers he provides are designed to direct us toward humility and away from sin, and the fact that these existential questions are raised at all shows how essential Akavia thinks they are to our inner lives. We *need* them. They should not be a source of angst or agony but a catalyst for moral and spiritual rectitude.

A few centuries after the compilation of *Pirke Avot*, the Babylonian Talmud interweaves a teaching from an important rabbinic sage with one of the less dreary sayings from Ecclesiastes—and once again, the Jewish tradition tries to view the relationship between death and life, mortality and morality, as symbiotic and beneficial:

> Rabbi Eliezer would say: "Repent one day before your death." His disciples asked: "Does a man know on which day he will die?" He said to them: "This being the case, he should repent today, for perhaps tomorrow he will die. In this way, all of his days will be passed in a state of repentance. Indeed, so said Kohelet in his wisdom: 'Your garments should always be white, and oil should never lack from your head.'" (BT Shabbat 153a)

What is most countercultural to me is that Rabbi Eliezer does not advocate that we indulge in temporal pleasures as our "last act" on the world's stage, but that we instead strive for *teshuvah*, for moral and spiritual renewal. And since we can never truly know which day will be our final one, the process of *teshuvah* should be a perpetual, lifelong pursuit. Kohelet appears in this passage as well. In a continuation of the verse cited above (Eccles. 9:8), the biblical king also says, "And a man cannot even know his time" (Eccles. 9:12). Rabbi Eliezer and Kohelet, while separated by time and geography, are actually "talking" to one another through the pages of the Talmud. Their focus on wearing white garments is significant, as it relates directly to the dynamic of repentance.

The white ritual garment that some Jewish men wear during the Days of Awe (known in Yiddish as a *kitel*) is meant to convey innocence, purity, vulnerability, and trust. It is designed to express—in an outward and visible way—our inner humility, our willingness to stand exposed before God on the sacred days of judgment. In traditional religious practice, Jewish men are both married *and* buried in them. When seen in this light, the *kitel* becomes a symbol of the human journey itself, a celebration of the New Year and the gift of life but also a death shroud, an acknowledgment of our mortality. Why not, as both sages urge us, wear it every day? Why not embrace the dialectic of death and life?

The nearness of death should not be a cause for despair, but a call to action.

White garments are not the only objects that bring to mind the psychospiritual connection between mortality and morality. So are skulls. Here is another provocative passage from *Pirke Avot*, attributed to the great sage Hillel: "He saw a skull floating on the surface of the water. He said to it: Because you drowned others, you were drowned; and those who drowned you, they themselves will [eventually] be drowned" (*Avot* 2:7).

This vivid and somewhat cryptic passage seems to convey a message about justice, about our actions and their consequences. If the skull belonged to a murderer, as Hillel suggests, then the punishment appears to fit the crime. The text further implies that the vicious cycle of crime and punishment will continue ad infinitum. Murder will beget more murder. For me, though, this passage raises some of the same questions that vex Kohelet. If sinner and saint, fool and sage, all face the same fate, what is the motivation for human beings to be good, or to be wise? Perhaps the notion of karmic justice that Hillel describes through the image of a floating skull relates specifically to premature and brutal death—not death itself, the great equalizer and unavoidable end for all of us.

The human skull is a potent symbol, and its presence transcends time and place. Art historians have noted that the theme of memento mori, or "remember you shall die," is very common in European paintings from the sixteenth and seventeenth centuries. In Christian art, images of Mary Magdalene regularly depict her contemplating a skull. It is also a common motif in fifteenth- and sixteenth-century British portraiture, where playful children or young men are often shown looking at skulls—jarring juxtapositions meant to highlight the transience of life. Skulls are familiar motifs in tombs, too.

One of the best-known illustrations of this image and theme occurs in a scene from *Hamlet*, a play that Shakespeare composed around this period. After a gravedigger exhumes the skull of a deceased court jester, the Danish prince exclaims,

> Alas, poor Yorick! I knew him, Horatio, a fellow of infinite jest, of most excellent fancy. He hath bore me on his back a thousand times, and now how abhorr'd in my imagination it is! My gorge rises at it. Here hung those lips that I have kissed I know not how oft. Where be your gibes now? (act 5, scene 1)

The contrast between the memory of a vivacious and dynamic Yorick ("a fellow of infinite jest, of most excellent fancy") and his still, silent remains is a dramatic representation of the philosophical theme of earthly vanity expressed earlier and so powerfully by Kohelet ("Utter futility! All is futile!"). If death is inescapable—according to what in the arts is known as the *vanitas* tradition—then our actions in life are ultimately inconsequential. The image of Hamlet meditating on the skull of Yorick has become, arguably, the most lasting creative embodiment of the classic *vanitas* idea.

It is an idea that we, like many others before us, must struggle with, heart and soul.

THE HAMLET MOMENT

When we confront the existential question of whether life is worth living—either because it feels unbearable (as in the case of Jeremiah) or because it seems meaningless (as in the mind of Kohelet)—we often find ourselves at what I call the "Hamlet Moment." Prior to the skull scene in Shakespeare's play, when the Danish prince finds himself in another dark mood about mortality, he recites the great soliloquy that has become perhaps the most famous in all of Western drama. Here is a large portion of it:

> To be, or not to be—that is the question:
> Whether 'tis nobler in the mind to suffer
> The slings and arrows of outrageous fortune
> Or to take arms against a sea of troubles
> And by opposing end them. To die, to sleep—
> No more—and by a sleep to say we end
> The heartache, and the thousand natural shocks
> That flesh is heir to. 'Tis a consummation
> Devoutly to be wished. To die, to sleep—
> To sleep—perchance to dream: ay, there's the rub,
> For in that sleep of death what dreams may come
> When we have shuffled off this mortal coil,
> Must give us pause. There's the respect
> That makes calamity of so long life. . . .
> Who would fardels bear,
> To grunt and sweat under a weary life,
> But that the dread of something after death,
> The undiscovered country, from whose bourn
> No traveller returns, puzzles the will,
> And makes us rather bear those ills we have
> Than fly to others that we know not of? (act 3, scene 1)

Hamlet begins his soliloquy on life and death with a question that, like other versions of the same inquiry we have explored in this chapter, lends itself to multiple interpretations. Hamlet is at his own existential crossroads, and he is in anguish. Yet there is debate as to what his words really mean. The prince is haunted by the killing of his father and pained by Ophelia's unrequited love for him. But is Hamlet actually expressing a suicidal desire, or is he just philosophizing on what death might bring?

Whatever his true intention, the prince clearly thinks that if we can endure the "slings and arrows" of the human condition, moving on with life is still a decision—which means we could choose the opposite, and end it. This is the Hamlet Moment, the crossroads many of us reach where we must weigh the challenges (yet familiarity) of being with the uncertainties (yet possibility) of nonbeing and then decide one way or another what course of action to take. For an existentialist philosopher like Jean-Paul Sartre (1905–80; author of *Being and Nothingness*), humans are "condemned" to this freedom. In the book of Deuteronomy, however, free will is viewed as a sacred gift, and we are given advice on which path we should choose: "I have set before you life and death, blessing and curse. Now choose life, so that you and your children may live" (Deut. 30:19).

Despite these ancient words of encouragement, it can be difficult to follow the Torah's directive. When life's "sea of troubles" makes us sometimes feel as if we are drowning, it is not always simple to choose life over death, being over nothingness.

As I described at the outset of this chapter, I have faced my own Hamlet Moment. And I consider myself fortunate to have survived it, in no small measure because of the courage exemplified by figures such as Jeremiah and Kohelet, whose tortured yet honest questions continue to resonate in contemporary minds and hearts as if they were voiced today.

While the fundamental inquiry into whether or not our lives are worth living has remained with us (and probably always will), the various related questions that are connected with it have changed over time, often reflective of developments in culture as well as of ever-evolving insights in psychology, sociology, ethics, and even biology:

Why do some people push through adversity and pain while others choose self-annihilation?

What internal and/or external factors account for these radically different outcomes?

Must we accept the fact of our existence rather than act, willfully, to bring about its termination?

Scholars, scientists, and seekers have tried to respond to these questions in many different ways, but each response usually results in the emergence of new and equally challenging questions and uncertainties.

In his novel *The Unnamable*, Samuel Beckett (1906–89) appears to capture the essence of humanity's ongoing, perplexing, sometimes heroic struggle between "a quest for immobility" and the persistent, sometimes unfathomable drive toward self-preservation:

> Perhaps it's done already, perhaps they have said me already, perhaps they have carried me to the threshold of my story, before the door that opens on my story, that would surprise me, if it opens, it will be I, it will be the silence, where I am, I don't know, I'll never know, in the silence you don't know, you must go on, I can't go on, I'll go on.

Each of our lives is a story, and we try to live our stories as best we can despite all of our limitations and challenges. Yet our stories are not always written with words. At times, it is silence and mystery that define our journeys. It was the silence of Sawtooth Mountain that pushed me forward when I stood at a threshold, and it was the mystery of my will to live that saved me when I stood at another. In the context of religious history, it is the ineffable dimensions of the Torah that, in my view, are among its most intriguing and life transforming.

Even when we don't know where we are or where exactly we are going—and, as Beckett suggests, that is all the time—we can go on because we *must* go on. When all seems lost, when the burden of our story seems too great for us to bear, our ungraspable drive to endure has the power to carry, preserve, and ultimately rescue us.

2

The Strong and Silent Type

MIDWAY THROUGH RABBINICAL SCHOOL, I had a summer intern-
ship with a small synagogue in Fairbanks, Alaska. I became friends that
summer with Dave, an environmental activist and wilderness guide who
raised sled dogs on the side. Dave wasn't Jewish or a member of the congregation, and it was always a welcome respite from my quasi-public role
and pulpit responsibilities when we hung out. Dave and I stayed out late
many nights under the light of the midnight sun, drinking beer and playing volleyball at a roadhouse called The Howling Dog, just north of town.

Dave lived off the grid with his dog Cody in a cabin on the outskirts
of Fairbanks. In a number of respects, I envied his situation. Dave had
no attachments, nothing to hold him down. Since he eked out a living
as a guide, Dave's time was more or less his own. While I'd always been
torn between the pleasures of radical freedom and the comforting bonds
(yet also constraints) of community, Dave had made a clear choice that
favored the former arrangement. He worked when he wanted to work,
and he was responsible for no person other than himself.

At my request, Dave taught me the basics of dog mushing before I
had to return to New York City to resume my studies. Since it was summer, we used a jerry-rigged ATV in place of a sled, and the dogs pulled us
down dirt roads much as they would when there was snow on the ground.
I learned the differences between lead, swing, and wheel dogs; how to
put on harnesses and attach tethers and static lines; what to do when
ascending and descending hills. While I'd ridden on horses many times,
I'd never before felt the unique sensation of being pulled by a powerful
team of huskies and malamutes.

I couldn't wait to mush "for real." I returned to Alaska that winter, and Dave and I took two dog teams on a five-day foray into the White Mountains, a starkly beautiful area north of Fairbanks. Virtually everything about that trip—from camping in the snow to making turns on my sled without falling off—was a challenge. But I was hooked on dog mushing. And I was especially hooked on mushing in the Far North.

It took another two years before I was able to make it back for a more intense and remote trip, this time in the wilderness of the Brooks Range, a majestic wedge of mountains that cuts across the northern half of Alaska and that is well north of the Arctic Circle. With the exception of a few mining and Native communities, the Brooks Range is mostly uninhabited, and it teems with wildlife: wolves, lynx, wolverines, Dall sheep, black bears, grizzlies, moose, and caribou that number in the scores of thousands.

I'd been an ordained rabbi for less than a year, and I was already struggling, both with the intense commitment involved in serving a congregation and with finding spiritual uplift in my chosen path. While it was a spiritual impulse that had motivated my decision to become a rabbi, after five years of training and a year in the field, my experience of Jewish professional life had been about as uninspiring as I could have imagined. I spent more time dealing with politics and self-entitled parents than I did focused on prayer, contemplation, or the existential needs of congregants. I had to get (far) away for a while—for my own sake, as well as for those men and women I might one day serve.

I had to find a new source of inspiration.

The day after I landed in Fairbanks, Dave and I loaded over a dozen barking dogs into the transport track above his truck, hauled and secured our two sleds over that, and drove north up the Dalton Highway, a road that extends all the way to the hulking oil-drilling rigs at Prudhoe Bay on the edge of the Arctic Ocean. Our starting point was near the mining camp of Nolan, about a twelve-hour drive from Fairbanks. We reached the camp at two in the morning. The dogs were silent. A few of the miners were still awake in one of their trailers (they had just finished their shift) and they invited us in to warm up. We spoke with them about mining, dogs, and the condition of the trail we were about to mush on. Then the two of us slept in the truck while our dogs slept to the side of the road, each one attached by its collar to the picket line that linked them together.

At dawn, after feeding our teams, Dave and I put on the dogs' harnesses and hooked them up to their respective sleds. Dave led the way to the trailhead at Wiseman Creek. I followed. Pulled by our fresh and excited dogs, both of our sleds careened off the road, barreled ahead another couple of hundred yards over taiga, then entered a wooded area. All traces of human civilization suddenly disappeared. We were mushing in Gates of the Arctic National Park, and the Brooks Range was just a subregion within the immense and spectacular swath of interior Alaska. I had never before been anywhere as remote or as dramatic, and the next week or so filled me with joy and inspiration.

Several days into our trip, on a Friday night, I tried to observe a make-shift Shabbat beneath the Endicott Mountains. I took out two candles I'd packed in New York and stuck them into the snow. After I said the proper blessings, Dave and I ate dinner, drank some rum by the campfire, and got ready to turn in when it grew dark. His dog Cody had joined us on the trip, and Cody positioned himself between our sleeping bags in the tent. Dave fell asleep right away, but I had to relieve myself at a nearby river.

As I walked down toward it, the dogs watched my every step. They were curled into balls to protect themselves from the cold. I was cold, too. And exhausted. I'd been so busy dealing with the day-to-day chores of handling my team that I'd largely forgotten what it was that had driven me to this wild and distant land in the first place. But as I stood there alone on the tundra and gazed over the peaks into the sky, I remembered.

The darkness ignited before me. Towering waves of white-green light scrolled across the heavens. It was the northern lights, the aurora borealis, a meteorological phenomenon related to Earth's magnetic field. I'd seen the lights before, but never like this. They seemed to be directly in front of me, flaming over the mountains. Almost beckoning. Pythagoras, the early Greek philosopher, claimed that the cosmos itself could speak, that the constant rotation of the celestial bodies was so great that they had to produce a noise. He called that sound the music of the spheres and argued that the reason human beings cannot hear it is that it has been with us since the very instant of birth, and we therefore have no way to distinguish it from its opposite, silence.

I heard something that night—not with my ears, but with my soul. I watched the aurora expand, contract, and pulsate above me, and it filled me with awe and amazement. It humbled me. It inspired me. And I knew then and there that I was in the presence of something wild, something ungraspable and unknowable. Transcendent and mysterious. Something that made me forget myself yet also experience so much *more* than myself.

I'd found what I'd come for.

"Who am I that I should go to Pharaoh?" (Exodus 3:11)

While Jeremiah, Kohelet, and so many others over the centuries have reflected on—and often agonized over—*why* we are, there are times in our lives when we are instead forced to ask ourselves *who* we are. The burning bush encounter in the third chapter of the book of Exodus triggers just such a situation for Moses. While he is tending the flock of his father-in-law, Moses receives a divine call. And like many of the biblical figures who follow him, Moses resists the charge to be a leader of his people. His resistance, however, is not rooted in concerns about the loneliness of his role or the heavy weight of leadership. In the view of many commentators, it is grounded in profound humility.

Is Moses a model for us all? Or is his example unrealistic and unattainable?

The Torah tells us that when Moses drives the sheep into the wilderness, he comes upon Mount Horeb. It is there that he witnesses a miraculous sight: "An angel of the LORD appeared to him in a blazing fire out of a bush. He gazed, and there was a bush all aflame, yet the bush was not consumed" (Exod. 3:2). Moses asks aloud, "Why doesn't the bush burn up?" (3:3). As he turns to get a better look, God speaks to him from the burning bush and warns him not to come any closer. The divine voice commands Moses to remove the sandals from his feet, for he stands on holy ground. After God says, "I am . . . the God of your father, the God of Abraham, the God of Isaac, and the God of Jacob," (3:6) Moses hides his face, fearful of looking at God, awed by the encounter.

His curiosity is transformed into fear and trembling. Moses listens silently as God explains the circumstances and then gives Moses his prophetic charge: God has marked well the plight of the Israelites in Egypt and has heeded their outcry; God is mindful of their sufferings; God will rescue them from their bondage and bring them to a land flowing with milk and honey. But God needs a human surrogate: "Come, therefore, I will send you to Pharaoh, and you shall free My people, the Israelites, from Egypt" (Exod. 3:10).

When Moses first sees the burning bush, he reacts with a question. When he now hears the call to lead his people out of slavery, Moses responds to God with another: "Who am I that I should go to Pharaoh and free the Israelites from Egypt?" (Exod. 3:11).

LOWERING THE BAR

Like Jeremiah, Moses is not very enthusiastic about his call to service. Both men initially offer words of protest to their respective charges, but the reason for Moses's reluctance is qualitatively different from that of the later prophet. Jeremiah feels oppressed by the isolation and scorn he experiences in the prophetic role, and his pain and despair ultimately drive him to question the value of life itself. For Moses, it is not a maelstrom of thoughts and feelings about mortality but rather a psycho-spiritual focus on his *identity* that fuels his protest and undergirds his question.

Who am I that I should go to Pharaoh? When people, institutions, or conditions compel us to take on the mantle of leadership—and force us to confront seemingly insurmountable obstacles—it can be a discomforting experience. When the call to lead comes directly from God, it can be even more challenging. Some run away from that challenge; others come to accept the leadership role, but with great resistance, even disdain, like Jeremiah. But there is a third response, and it is exemplified by Moses, through words of radical humility.

When called by God, Moses doesn't question the order. He questions himself.

Rashi (1040–1105), the great medieval commentator, interprets Moses's query as an expression of his fundamental uncertainty—and doubt—about his humble position in the world. "Who am I," writes Rashi in the voice of Moses, "that I am important enough to speak with kings?" Rashbam (1085–1158), an important interpreter (and a grandson of Rashi), gives more specificity: "Who am I? Am I then of sufficient status, a stranger like me to enter the court of a king?" At this point in the Exodus story, Moses, a non-Egyptian who has hidden his Hebrew identity, is on the run and hiding in the desert, after slaying an Egyptian taskmaster.

Moses's question goes far beyond his concerns about his social and political status; he questions his existential status as well. In the presence of God, and gripped by the first moments of the prophetic call, Moses can't help but wonder why God has chosen *him* to lead the Israelites from slavery to freedom. What has Moses done to merit God's attention? Moses takes off his sandals, shields his eyes, questions his own worthiness as a leader and his significance as a man. God does not address his unworthiness or insignificance. God's response to Moses is instead, "I will be with you" (Exod. 3:12).

So who exactly is Moses? Is he a great leader and an invaluable human being, or is he just a cog in the sweep of cosmic history? There is a spiritual tension in both the Bible and the later rabbinic tradition on these matters, not just for Moses, but for other key figures and leaders as well. For instance, Abraham, who boldly challenges God's judgment and capacity for mercy during the Sodom and Gomorrah episode, says about himself elsewhere, "I . . . am but dust and ashes" (Gen. 18:27). And David, who defeats a giant, commands an army, and rules an empire, exclaims with dramatic and stark self-deprecation, "I am a worm, less than human" (Ps. 22:7).

Abraham and David, like all humanity, are born in the image of God. Yet they, like Moses, distinguish themselves from most other people in the way that they *perceive* themselves. While they are patriarchs, kings, and prophets, they are also acutely aware of where they stand and who they are: flesh-and-blood creatures bound by limitations.

This self-perception, which is grounded in humility and indicative of identity, is found in other stories and through other teachings. And it is not limited to luminaries.

Rabbi Simcha Bunim of Peshischa (1765–1827), an important Hasidic master from Poland, taught that all people should dress in clothing that has two pockets, with a note in each pocket, so that we can reach into one or the other, depending on our need. When we feel low, disconsolate, or weary, we should reach into the right pocket and pull out the slip of paper that reads, "For my sake the world was created." But when we feel high and mighty, confident and secure, we should take out the paper in the left pocket that reads, "I am but dust and ashes."

All of us are mortal—and yet, all of us are also divinely exalted. When we've been brought low, we should remind ourselves that we are images of God. When we feel on top of the world, we should remember that we will eventually die. This teaching urges us to see the duality of our being rather than the (false) dichotomy in it. And it suggests that such a perspective will lead to balance and inner peace, protecting us from the dangers of self-destructiveness *and* the seductions of self-idolatry.

Yet how many of us have achieved the emotional equanimity that Rabbi Simcha Bunim advocates? For me, a man struggling through the middle years of life's journey, serenity and stability are more elusive than ever. Still, I think that is the point of the teaching. No living thing—and certainly no human being—exists in a state of stasis. Identity evolves. Who we are and how we perceive ourselves change over time. The variables that help to create (and constantly *re*-create) our personalities and characters are numerous: time, place, events, relationships. Every stage of life presents us with new challenges and new opportunities for growth—if our attitude is sound and we are ready.

The psychoanalyst Erik Erikson (1902–94) bases his theory of personality development on just such an idea. He argues that human beings pass through eight developmental stages over the course of a lifetime. In every one, a person confronts, and hopefully masters, a new challenge or conflict. Each stage is characterized by a psychosocial "crisis" of two conflicting forces (e.g., trust versus mistrust, intimacy versus isolation). When we reconcile these forces and resolve their associated conflicts, we evolve. When we fail to resolve them, we experience an identity crisis.

Erikson does not think that maturity and growth are automatic. We have to *work* for them, and that work often involves a balancing act: overconfidence can lead to false starts; timidity can lead to stagnation. If we are open, however, as well as resolute and appropriately well-adjusted, then progress and even wisdom are attainable for all of us.

Who am I? may be the question that Moses asks before he approaches Pharaoh, but that same attitude of introspection—and heartfelt, humble self-assessment—is necessary whenever human beings face challenges, be they internal or external in nature.

The Jewish custom of "sitting shivah" after the death of a loved one is widespread and ancient. In many traditional Jewish homes, mourners literally sit (on stools, pillows, or the floor) as they receive visitors during the seven-day period of grieving following the burial. This ritual act of placing oneself physically low to the ground creates a pose of humility. It also engenders a mind-set of reflection: we become more aware of our (spatial?) relationship to others, our feelings of sorrow and loss, our proximity to death.

As I discussed in the first chapter, an awareness of our mortality can trigger powerful emotions and intense contemplation. One effect that relates to heart as well as to head is humility. When Moses asks God, "Who am I?," he conveys both what he *feels* and who he *is*. The transcendent nature of the burning bush catalyzes his experiences of inspiration and revelation. Like a great work of art, it humbles and transforms his soul.

The life of Saint Francis of Assisi (1181–1226), and the tradition of Franciscan piety that followed him, led to a compelling genre of creative work that interweaves art with religion and inspiration with revelation. The "Madonna of humility" paintings were initially used by Franciscans to help them with their spiritual practice, specifically contemplation. In the convention of the genre, the Virgin Mary sits on the ground or on a low cushion, commonly holding a baby Jesus in her lap. Purposeful rather than artistic in intent (i.e., instilling in monks an attitude of reverence and devotion), this style of painting spread quickly throughout Italy. By the late fourteenth century, it began to appear in Spain, France, and Germany, a popular genre of the early Renaissance.

The word "humility" derives from the Latin root *humus*, meaning earth or ground. It is something low—or that lowers us. The Madonna of humility tradition, like the practice of sitting shivah, concretizes this metaphysical idea through creative and ritual expression. By taking us down (literally and figuratively, on cushions and stools or via a visual image), humility also "grounds" us. In making us descend, humility anchors our souls.

There is a concept in Kabbalah called *yeridah lifney ha-aliyah*, "descent before ascent." For the Jewish mystics, a journey down into our existential muck and mire is viewed as a sacred rite of passage. When we encounter a challenge—whether it is a charge to face Pharaoh or the death of a loved one—we can either let it cripple us or humbly seek its lessons and boldly move forward. Descent is only the preparation for ascent. In the Torah, Egypt—geographically lower than the land of Canaan—often serves as a metaphor for that descent. A famine drives Abraham there. Joseph, thrown into a pit by his jealous brothers, is taken there by Midianite traders. And Moses is born in and must return to Egypt, a land of pain and suffering for his people and the scene of his crime.

The mystics reread the word *mitzraim* not as the historical Egypt, but as "straights" (*metzarim*), obstacles and ordeals that must be overcome. Abraham leaves Egypt for the land of milk and honey and sets into motion the birth of a nation; Moses leaves it for the wilderness of Sinai and the theophany of the burning bush. Even Joseph, who lives out his life in Egyptian exile, has his bones gathered and "taken up" with the Israelites during their exodus from the land of bondage to the Promised Land. All three figures, in different ways, are ultimately triumphant over their respective *metzarim*. Their experiences of descent are not permanent. Their challenges don't paralyze their souls; they elevate them. As a result, Abraham, Moses, and Joseph transform into great leaders.

As the idea of *yeridah*, descent, implies, humility is not about self-debasement, but self-*definition*. How we choose to assess our abilities and respond to life's trials largely determines our characters. When we find ourselves traveling through our own "Egypt," will we succumb to fear, anxiety, and despair, or will we instead submit our souls to the higher power guiding our steps? It is critically important to know our capabilities—but it is equally essential that we understand our human limitations. Saint Thomas Aquinas (1225–74), the towering Scholastic philosopher and theologian, defines humility in *Summa contra Gentiles* as a spiritual virtue that "consists in keeping oneself within one's own bounds, not reaching out to things above oneself, but submitting to one's superior."

For most contemporary men and women, the notion of submitting ourselves to anything or anyone is completely discordant—and for many, it is downright offensive. Yet "hierarchy" is not a four-letter word. The only way we mature as human beings is in relationship with others, and by trusting and learning from those who know more than we do. As Aquinas writes, the way we grow in the spiritual context is through humble submission to a "superior," which, taken to its logical extension, implies submission to that transcendent reality that is above all other realities (i.e., God). Humility is not about giving up, but giving over; an act of spiritual maturity, humility means voluntarily *choosing* to accept our limitations and then "bowing" before the Boundless One.

While this may be a countercultural idea today, it is certainly not a new one. The Abrahamic faith traditions all extol the significance of, and the need for, spiritual submission. A committed Jew must freely put on the "yoke" of God's sovereignty (*ol ha-malchut* in Hebrew) through ethical and ritual observance. A devoted Christian imitates the behavior of Jesus whenever that person places the moral and spiritual weight of the "cross" on his or her own shoulders. And an individual who practices Islam (an Arabic word that means submission) becomes worthy of the name "Muslim" (one who submits) only if that person chooses to "bend" his or her will to make it align with God's.

Humility opens the path to both spiritual descent and spiritual submission. It is a psychological attitude, and a religious virtue, that helps us to define who we are—and who we are not. While humility "lowers" the soul, it does so only in order to lift it.

Self-effacement, not self-denigration, is the hallmark of humility. When we ask ourselves, "Who am I?" (to confront adversity, to take on the mantle of leadership, to engage in a relationship with God), we acknowledge our limitations and affirm a reality higher than us—but we also affirm the self we have received and that we continue to develop. In light of the mysteries and complexities of life, it is a self that we must keep in proper perspective. While each one of us possesses a spark of the divine within our souls, we are also made from dust and ashes. The truly humble person, ever-conscious of this sober yet sublime dialectic, knows that while human beings are capable of great actions and monumental achievements, the glory ultimately belongs to God alone.

When selected for a special purpose, elevated in status, or lauded with praise, those who follow the model of Moses will know when it is appropriate to express gratitude for our merits and when it is better, and more fitting, to stay silent and push our egos completely aside.

BEING AND NOTHINGNESS

Moses is a Rorschach test for religious thinkers and spiritual seekers. The ways in which the faithful describe (and project qualities on) him often say more about them than they do about the biblical prophet. For the rabbis, he is Moshe Rabbeinu, a rabbi and a learned teacher. For Maimonides, Moses is a philosopher, a staunch rationalist, and a wise metaphysician. For Jewish mystics, Moses is a man who has reached the summit of spiritual prowess, a mystic with a direct, ongoing experience of divine communion.

Moses raises the bar on personal rectitude through his humility and self-effacing sense of identity. The mystics, however, are not interested in a purely characterological approach to Moses. They, like the rabbis and Maimonides, see in the figure of Moses a reflection of themselves. He is what they aspire to be, the actualization of their ideals.

One of the most influential and compelling mystics in the early Hasidic movement was Rabbi Dov Baer of Mezeritch (who died in 1772). Dov Baer, also known as the Great Maggid (great preacher), writes extensively about *unio mystica*, the mystical encounter with God. For the Maggid, the experience of "nothingness" (*ayin* in Hebrew) is the spiritual portal through which the mystic comes to commune with the divine. As he writes in *Maggid D'varav l'Yaakov*,

One must think of oneself as *ayin* and forget oneself totally.... Then one can transcend time, rising to the world of thought, where all is equal: life and death, ocean and dry land.... Such is not the case when one is attached to the corporeal nature of this world.... If one thinks of oneself as something, then the Holy One, blessed be He, cannot clothe Himself in [the mystic], for He is the Infinite One, and no vessel can withstand Him, unless one thinks of oneself as *ayin*.

Since God's nature is infinite and incorporeal, a mystic can make the space in which God may enter only if the mystic *him- or herself* transcends the material world. To consider oneself as "something" (i.e., to have an identity) is to think of oneself as a substantial being—yet no material vessel can ever hold that which is, in its essential nature, immaterial. To make room for God, the mystic must "forget" him- or herself or think of him- or herself as nothing. Rather than self-effacing humility, mystical forgetting results in self-*negation*. And it is through self-negation, or the dissolution of one's ego and identity, that the mystic provides the emptiness in which God can dwell.

Moses is the paradigm for this mystical encounter with the Infinite One. The Maggid continues,

> We find a distinction among the righteous: Abraham said "I am but dust and ashes," and David said "I am a worm, and no man." These men both [still claim] a degree of existence. But Moses asked "What are we?" (Exod. 16:7) [This means that] he was in a state of *ayin*, as it is written, "Now Moses was a very humble man, more so than any other man on earth." (Num. 12:3) He therefore understood the divine essence, which is not the case with rest of the prophets who came before or after him.

Moses's question "Who am I that I should go to Pharaoh?" has served as the springboard for this chapter and allowed us to explore issues of character, personal growth, and identity. The Maggid expands on this question by citing another one that Moses asks later in the book of Exodus: "What are we that you should grumble against us?" (Exod. 16:7). In its context, Moses (accompanied by his brother Aaron) chastises the Israelites for challenging their leadership. Yet the Maggid focuses only on the first part of the question, "What are we?," as he compares Moses to both Abraham and David.

While masters of humility, Abraham and David still retain a sense of self-consciousness. They may see themselves as dust, ashes, and worms, but they still have discrete identities. Moses, on the other hand, questions the very *idea* of his existence. If he has no material reality (in the mystical state), then how can he have an identity or a personality? The Maggid interprets the question "What are we?" as illustrative of the fact that Moses does not consider himself to be even dust. His words indicate that he, unlike Abraham and David, has reached a state of *ayin*, or nothingness. For the Maggid, *ayin* is the only state of mind appropriate for one who seeks to become a divine vessel.

Nothingness, in the mystical context, is the collapse of self-consciousness, the disintegration of individual identity that results from a brush with divinity. Moses's first question ("Who am I?") shows that he is on the path toward divine communion. But his second question ("What are we?") informs us that he has experienced it firsthand.

Fear, more than humility, often accompanies self-negation. The Maggid compares the dynamic of mystical communion to a candle placed before a torch: just as a candle is useless and unable to function in an identifiable way if it is too close to the torch, so are the capacities—and identity—of a person wiped out while in the awe-inspiring presence of God. The fear that is part of this fleeting encounter negates not only the person's other thoughts and emotions but also his or her sense of self.

At the moment of communion, according to the Maggid, a "fire of silence" descends on the mystic and a "great fear" grips that person's soul. The mystic cannot see or hear. The mystic no longer knows where he or she is or even who he or she is. In this state of ecstasy, the border between the material and the spiritual dimension blurs.

What are we? may be the only question that is proper, or even possible, to ask.

Not long after the Maggid died, the existentialist thinker Søren Kierkegaard (1813–55) was born. While he was separated from the Maggid by both geography and religion, Kierkegaard's work reveals intellectual leanings that many refer to as "mystical." He argues that only through our willingness to make a leap into radical uncertainty and adopt an attitude of "infinite resignation" about our capacity to understand an ineffable, transcendent God will we be able to evolve as spiritual beings. For Kierkegaard, that leap of faith is an expression of deep humility as well as of profound strength. Though an act of spiritual submission, it is also an act of forceful assertion, an affirmation—through quiet acceptance—of our limited humanity.

The reality of a transcendent God, a God who is untouchable, elusive, beyond us, rests at the core of Kierkegaard's thought. He writes in *The Sickness unto Death* that there is "a deep gulf of qualitative difference" between divinity and humanity, between the Infinite and the finite. While human beings are situated in the realm of existence, God resides in the sphere of the limitless and the eternal, completely independent of the world. We are different from God, not just with regard to capacities, such as power or life span, but in *kind*. Like the Maggid, Kierkegaard posits that only an indirect and mediated relationship with God is possible. For the Maggid, it is the experience of *ayin* and self-negation that creates the space for divine-human contact. For Kierkegaard, it is a leap of faith and self-resignation (along with an experience of existential awe) that leads to the encounter with transcendent reality.

The radical gulf of qualitative difference between humanity and God is most obvious in the area of the mind. Kierkegaard urges us to withdraw our confidence in and reliance on the faculty of reason, since reason will never be capable of understanding the divine, of grasping what is fundamentally different from itself. The great paradox of rational thought is, as he writes in *Philosophical Fragments*, that it wants "to discover something that thought itself cannot think." The unknown (and unknowable) reality that the mind confronts as it strives for insight is none other than God, the divine mystery and "absolute frontier."

When we try to define God, we treat God as an object, a thing. This interferes with, and distances us from, our relationship with divinity. That is why, during the burning bush episode, Moses does not receive a clear and direct answer when he asks for God's name. God simply replies, *Ehyeh-Asher-Ehyeh*, "I am who I am" (Exod. 3:14).

Kierkegaard is not concerned (as is the Maggid) with the question "What are we?" and instead seems to be far more interested in the opposite question: "What are we not?" As finite and limited material beings, we are certainly *not God*, but that knowledge can help us to better grasp—and reconstruct—our own identities after the experience of self-resignation, an experience that can be transformational.

For Kierkegaard, infinite resignation is an act of the will, not the mind. So is faith. As a result, faith is not and cannot be a permanent state, a sustained, comfortable place of rest. It is a constant struggle, a fight, the ultimate state of tension. Faith must be renewed perpetually, again and again, and very few of us are capable of such a feat. That is why only a warrior, a "knight of faith," is able to confront this challenge. Through strength of will and fierce determination, only one of truly heroic faith can stare into the face of radical mystery and believe nonetheless. And do it again, over and over and over.

Who are we . . .
  What are we . . .
    . . . that we should strive to know an unknowable God?

Inspired by Moses's questions, Kierkegaard and the Maggid develop spiritual systems very much in accord with the long-standing theological tradition of *via negativa*. The central idea of this tradition (also known as negative theology) is that human beings can never know who or what God is, only who or what God is *not*. One of the masterworks of negative theology is *The Cloud of Unknowing*, an anonymous and influential work of Christian mysticism written toward the end of the fourteenth century.

The text is a guide for a young student and spiritual seeker. It counsels the student to seek God, not through preconceived notions or the faculty of reason, but through intense and loving contemplation. The student is told that he may come to know God only when he strips away all thoughts and desires and gives himself over to the "cloud of forgetting." The cloud of forgetting (like the Maggid's concept of *ayin*) dissolves his sense of self and allows him to enter the nearly impervious "cloud of unknowing." It is in this realm of "unknowingness" that he may glimpse God's nature. *The Cloud of Unknowing* states,

> For [God] can well be loved, but he cannot be thought. By love he can be grasped and held, but by thought, neither grasped nor held.

And therefore, though it may be good at times to think specifically of the kindness and excellence of God, and though this may be a light and a part of contemplation, all the same, in the work of contemplation itself, it must be cast down and covered with a cloud of forgetting. And you must step above it stoutly but deftly, with a devout and delightful stirring of love, and struggle to pierce that darkness above you; and beat on that thick cloud of unknowing with a sharp dart of longing love, and do not give up, whatever happens.

In the mystical context, "knowledge" of God arises not from cognition, but from feeling, the result of contemplation, meditation, prayer. It is only through struggle and persistence that the "dart of longing love" can pierce the cloud of unknowing. Even then, only an indirect experience of God is possible. The cloud of unknowing is the veil—and eternal boundary—that separates the human mind from God's true nature. While the images and metaphors that are used to describe this veil may vary (a burning bush, an ineffable name, a thick cloud, or even the northern lights), the message of Scripture and many of the mystical and theological teachings that follow it are consistent: even though God's essence and identity are forever beyond our grasp, it is possible for us to *brush* against transcendence.

STRENGTH IN SMALLNESS

At times, there are experiences and events in our lives that force us to call into question not only who we are, but what we are. Perhaps, like Moses in the story of the burning bush, we find ourselves chosen for a position of leadership that seems far beyond our abilities. Or perhaps, through a mystical encounter (or a meteorological event), we actually lose our sense of self in the presence of a greater reality. While disconcerting, the feelings of humility and self-negation that can accompany such episodes are also powerful catalysts for transformation. If we are receptive to it, the experience of being made "small" can lead to newfound strength of character and spiritual empowerment.

In the spiritual context, inner strength often emanates from places we don't ordinarily expect it to. Yet it is precisely, and paradoxically, in the areas of submission, vulnerability, and openness that we can find some of our deepest reservoirs of internal power. The Hebrew word "Kabbalah," for instance, one of the great mystical movements, means "that which is received." To put it another way, authentic spiritual experience—and the transformative capacities that are linked to it—is something that *comes* to us, not something that we can go out and "get." It is the result of giving over, not of giving up.

Moses asks profound existential questions (*Who am I? What are we?*) that reveal his doubts about his abilities, his confusion about his identity, and his perplexity about the place of humanity in the cosmic context. They also reveal, implicitly and indirectly, both the dimensions and the limitations of the relationship between God and human beings, a relationship marked by intimacy but ultimately bound by unknowability.

Moses can be viewed through many lenses.

In the eyes of most biblical commentators, Moses is a man of strength and purpose, a leader of exceptional, even singular character: "Now Moses was a very humble man, more so than any other man on earth" (Num. 12:3).

In the eyes of the Jewish mystics and other religious thinkers, Moses is a spiritual master—the Maggid's paradigmatic mystic, Kierkegaard's knight of faith.

Moses is a man of action, not words. When he kills an Egyptian who is beating a fellow Hebrew, Moses dispatches him without saying a single thing. And before he accepts the mantle of leadership in order to free his people from their bondage, Moses informs God, "Please, O Lord, I have never been a man of words, either in times past or now that You have spoken to Your servant; I am slow of speech and slow of tongue" (Exod. 4:10).

Over and above his great deeds, however, and despite this declaration about his lack of verbal gifts, Moses essentially functions as the mouthpiece for God throughout four of the five books that constitute the Torah. Verse after verse depicts Moses speaking to the people of Israel, guiding them, consoling them, castigating them, at times "singing" to them (near the end of his life, in Deuteronomy, chapter 32). Moses's humility is more than exceptional—it is *radical*. And it only reinforces his worthiness as a leader and appropriateness as the challenger to Pharaoh.

When Moses asks God, "Who am I that I should go to Pharaoh?," his radical humility signals—and serves as an overlay for—the intensity of his strength and courage. These are the very qualities that, in the view of many commentators, play such a critical role in Moses's election as a leader in the first place, and they show how his moral and spiritual power arises from a place that is deep, quiet, and small. Maybe Moses's special relationship with God is the animating force behind his power. And maybe that bond is what transforms and amplifies his "still, small voice" into a vessel for the divine message.

During a constricting and almost soulless period in my life, I found inspiration in Alaska, through the northern lights. More than the objective beauty of the aurora, however, it was how its lights made me forget myself, how the power of the natural phenomenon humbled and reignited my soul, that relates to Moses's question. As a result of my experience in the Arctic, I was able to return to my life as a rabbi with renewed commitment and passion—not necessarily for my people, but for the God we worshipped. I would have other experiences that would challenge that commitment (and I still do), but the memory of the aurora has never left me, and it reminds me that I have not made a mistake, that my calling was real and for a reason.

At different points and in different ways, we will all have to traverse our inner *metzarim*, those narrow places that threaten to confine and constrain us. And we will inevitably have to face our own pharaohs as well, those persons or forces that seek to oppress or harm us. These challenges will almost certainly cause us to question our ability and resolve. But there is hope. With Moses as our model of courage and strength, as the very embodiment of moral leadership and spiritual mastery, there will always be something to strive for, something to yearn to become, something that resembles victory.

3

Rules, Regs, and Rebellion

TOWARD THE END OF MY time living in New York City, and before I moved to Chicago to try to build a new life and career, I met frequently with one family from my congregation. While I was in professional and personal limbo—with one foot planted in the work that had shaped my identity for a decade and the other one increasingly out the door—it was the relationship with that family that grounded me and gave me a sense of moral duty. The situation, while tragic, was also transformative. I'd become so disillusioned about religious community, about the lack of commitment shown to their faith tradition by most of those I was serving, that I needed a concrete example of what religious work could do, or at least be, at its best.

I needed to see how religion, and a religious vocation, could help bring people closer rather than drive them apart.

The Diamonds were one of the founding families of our synagogue. I had gotten to know all four of them over the years through religious school, bar mitzvahs, retreats, and adult learning programs. The husband, Bill, was a very successful architect, and the wife, Susan, had worked in investment banking before deciding to leave it behind and focus her time on volunteer work and raising her two boys. The family was active in the congregation and consistently supportive of our financial needs.

I counted them as my friends.

We first got to know one another more intimately during a congregational retreat at a camp in the Connecticut Berkshires. The context helped to create informal and positive interactions, whether it was during meals in the dining hall, reading and discussing the Torah on a hillside, or playing softball. Bill, who was not a big talker (which was anomalous in this group of intense and boisterous Manhattanites), became animated on the ball field. He was tall and athletic, and I have vivid memories of watching him drive softballs deep into the outfield with a seemingly effortless swing.

While he did not show up very often to services or synagogue events, I always enjoyed his presence and (quietly charismatic) personality when he did. The Diamonds lived in Tribeca. After the collapse of the World Trade Center on 9/11, and because of their apartment's proximity to Ground Zero and the noxious gases that emanated from it, Bill and his family had to move out and live with various friends for several months. I checked in with them frequently and tried to offer support during their dislocation from home.

Not long after they had moved back to Tribeca, I was notified by my lay leadership that Bill had been diagnosed with Lou Gehrig's disease, or ALS, a neurological disease that has no cure. While, as a young rabbi, I had seen my share of challenging situations (and had served, in fact, as a chaplain to first responders and members of law enforcement at Ground Zero in the days immediately after the terrorist attack), bearing witness to Bill's rapid, inexorable decline and extreme motor degeneration was something that I had never before encountered.

It seemed almost unfathomable to me that such a horrific disease, following so closely on the family's prior trauma and disruption, could strike a good, honest man in his prime, and ultimately affect his entire household, so arbitrarily and irrevocably.

It was like a chapter from the book of Job.

I visited Bill and his family regularly. Everyone did their best to stay hopeful, but after many and varied consultations and treatments, Bill, Susan, and their kids braced for the inevitable. Over several months, I watched helplessly as the disease quickly and viciously attacked Bill: he went from walking with a cane, to sitting in a wheelchair, to being confined to a bed. In our private moments, Bill cried about his constantly deteriorating condition and his concern about the future of his wife and children. He expressed his doubts about God. He shared memories from his past and fears about what was to come. Bill's voice grew weaker by the week; it was often very challenging just to understand the words he would whisper, barely audibly, into my ear.

I felt profound sadness. And I felt inadequate to the task.

Mostly, I just listened. My job, as I saw it, wasn't to teach or guide—it was to be there for Bill and his family. I practiced what some call the "ministry of presence." Sitting by the bedside. Touching Bill's shoulder.

Soon, Bill could no longer speak at all. I began spending more time with Susan and the kids than with Bill himself. The family was devastated. The oldest son was leaving for college in the fall and the younger one was in high school. Neither child could speak to me without crying. Susan struggled to keep herself together and shared her thoughts about the next steps for herself and the boys. The three of them weren't just entering a new chapter, she said. They were embarking on a completely new life.

After Bill died and I officiated at the funeral, I reflected on the role that he and his family had played (and still play) in my life. Despite my ambivalence about working as a pulpit rabbi, my relationship with the Diamonds—and the experience of trying to help them through their harrowing journey—reminded me of the great responsibility of my vocation, and the possibility it offered me to give my presence, and support, to those who are struggling. Only a religious community possessed that sort of power. Only a spiritual bond could bring total strangers that close to, and make them responsible for, one another.

While my own chapter with the synagogue was coming to a close, I could think of few other career paths that would provide me with the opportunity to enter the life of a family and to strive for positive and lasting impact on the individuals within it.

It has been several years since I have worked as the spiritual leader of a congregation. There is a lot that I do not miss in the slightest—the overall lack of commitment, the internal politics, the sense of entitlement, the overemphasis on bar and bat mitzvahs. What I do miss, however, and what I miss greatly, is having the platform and entry point to serve and comfort those who are in need. I have worked in other contexts since my interactions with the Diamonds, but none of them have been as meaningful or made me feel as connected to a moral universe. And I wonder if the price I have to pay for participating in such a fulfilling world is to accept imperfection.

"Am I my brother's keeper?" (Genesis 4:9)

As I noted in the introduction, some of the questions I explore in this book are famous and some are infamous. The one that this chapter centers on is both. The question that Cain uses to answer God after God enquires into the whereabouts of Cain's brother, Abel, is arguably one of the best known and most broadly referenced in the Bible. It is usually linked with the theme of personal responsibility—our obligations toward fellow human beings and the implicit social contract on which civilization is built.

The fourth chapter of Genesis depicts a world that has just been created. Adam and Eve have been expelled from the Garden of Eden, blocked from reentry to the east by cherubim and a fiery, swirling sword. The first man and first woman give birth to the world's first children, Cain and Abel. The older brother, Cain, is a farmer, while the younger one, Abel, is a shepherd. Each sibling makes an offering to God. For a reason that is not explained, God accepts Abel's offering and rejects Cain's. Cain is bewildered and enraged. When the two brothers are in a field together, Cain kills Abel.

In verse nine, God asks Cain where his brother is. Cain's retort is, "I do not know." Then Cain asks, *hashomer achi anochi,* which in the JPS translation reads, "Am I my brother's keeper?"

And that seals his fate—not just in the story, but in Western thought, literature, and art. Cain is a murderer (the world's first), a model of depravity, a monster.

Or is he? Do Cain, and his infamous question, really warrant the vitriol and harsh judgments that have been associated with them over the centuries? There have been voices of dissent to the dominant (and negative) view almost from the start. As some commentators have pointed out, Cain's three-word reply can only be properly understood, and then thoughtfully evaluated, if we first take into account a wide range of other important factors, such as context, diction, even inflection.

According to the text, Adam and Eve are never "born." They are primeval (and semidivine?) beings fashioned by God, respectively, from the earth and from a rib. They are also immortal—at least at first. It is only with the story of Cain and Abel that the Bible begins to capture the nature of what it means to be fully human. The two siblings are conceived by human parents, they work, and they perform acts of religiosity. These are all firsts. Yet perhaps the most important first in this tale is the appearance of death, and the fact that the first death in human history is caused by an act of murder.

Cain's infamous question in the aftermath of that murder must be explored in depth before we can address the topic of personal responsibility more generally.

REBEL WITHOUT A CAUSE

The standard interpretation of Cain's reply to God is that his intent and attitude are sarcastic and rebellious. Rather than telling God the truth about what happened to Abel, Cain feigns ignorance and performs an act of verbal judo by asking his counterquestion. Cain's words do not relate to his brother's location, but to Cain's own role. The world he lives in is virtually unpopulated. God has established no covenant yet nor handed down any rules or regulations that govern human behavior. In this context, why shouldn't Cain follow his impulses and just do whatever he wants?

We will never know exactly how Cain pronounced the words *hashomer achi anochi*. His very inflection might have helped to reveal his true intent (as I will discuss later in the chapter). Still, it is significant that the first word of his question, and its placement within the Hebrew construction of the response, is *shomer*.

What is a *shomer*? The JPS Tanakh translates it as "keeper." But the word can be translated in other ways. It can mean guardian, defender, shield, sentinel, someone who has the "back" of another. The JPS version fails to capture the word's many nuances. I offer three alternatives to "Am I my brother's keeper?" that, in my view, convey three different aspects of its meaning:

1. "Am I the *custodian* of my brother?"
2. "Am I the *protector* of my brother?"
3. "Am I the *watchman* of my brother?"

In the first version, Cain asks God if Abel has been entrusted into his personal care, if it is his job to tend to his brother's well-being and nurture his growth.

In the second version, Cain asks if he is supposed to be Abel's defender, his human shield against potential attack and injury.

In the third version, Cain asks God if his role is to watch over his brother, to maintain a state of perpetual vigilance against any and all forces out to harm him.

Cain lives in a world in which much is unknown and threatening. As God warns him ominously in verse seven, "Sin crouches at the door." Regardless of which version of his question Cain means, serving as a *shomer* for Abel would entail an enormous amount of responsibility. Cain doesn't want to accept such a huge burden. His terse and somewhat cryptic reply to God is almost always associated with defiance and rebellion. In his rejection of responsibility (and, by implication, a moral order), Cain is viewed by most as the archetypal embodiment of nihilism.

Rashi interprets God's question ("Where is your brother Abel?") as a rhetorical device, a way to give Cain a last chance to confess his crime; God asks the question "to engage him with gentle words, [so that] perhaps he would repent and say, 'I have killed him and sinned against you.'" But Cain does not show remorse. He does not acknowledge his deed. And he lies to God. This prompted Rabbi J. H. Hertz (1872–1946), a former chief rabbi of Britain, to write in his Torah commentary, "Cain's answer is both false and insolent. Only a murderer altogether renounces the obligations of brotherhood."

Viewed through the lens of the normative rabbinic tradition, Cain is much more than a liar. He is a sociopath.

In one imagining of the killing (from Midrash Tanhuma), Cain is depicted as so determined to take his brother's life that his actions seem devoid of emotion and conscience. This chilling portrait of Cain makes him come across as detached, almost clinical, in his lethality: "How did he slay his brother? Cain took a stone and inflicted many contusions and bruises on Abel's arms and legs, for he did not know what part of the body out of which the soul is released, until, when he got to his neck, Abel died."

Cain's behavior raises a question: is he *amoral* or *immoral*? Does Cain live in a world in which he does not feel bound by the call of a moral system, or does he accept that a system of good and evil exists but choose to break its rules anyway?

Cain's father, Adam, is very clearly directed by God to be the *shomer* of the Garden of Eden (Gen. 2:15). In contrast, Cain never receives a parallel directive to be the *shomer* of his brother, Abel. Yet God's angry reaction following Abel's murder suggests that Cain should have intuited as much. But how? Is it because his parents ate the fruit from the Tree of the Knowledge of Good and Evil? Was Cain supposed to have inherited a moral compass through his DNA? God never answers this question directly.

This much is clear: by killing his brother, Cain fails to step into his role as Abel's *shomer* and instead becomes the very agent who brings about Abel's intentional and violent death. Whether or not there is a moral code at this primeval stage of the human journey, it is left unspoken in the biblical text. Still, Abel's silence is deafening: "What have you done? Hark, your brother's blood cries out to Me from the ground!" (Gen. 4:10).

Cain's deed has reverberated through the centuries. While his actions are deeply troubling and the fodder for much discussion, the punishment that he receives from God is, arguably, just as disturbing and worthy of examination. Following Cain's act of fratricide, God does not exact retribution for Abel by taking Cain's life as well. Instead, God proclaims a curse: "Therefore, you shall be more cursed than the ground, which opened its mouth to receive your brother's blood from your hand. If you till the soil, it shall no longer yield its strength to you. You shall become a ceaseless wanderer on earth" (Gen. 4:11–12).

Adam and Eve may have been expelled from Eden for their crime, but Cain is banished from the earth itself. The same soil that once nourished him as a farmer will now, as the result of his defilement of it with Abel's blood, become the source of his agony as a fugitive and nomad. Cain is condemned to wander, never finding rest, never finding a home. We must assume that this is a punishment without an endpoint, a curse meant to last forever. There is no mention of Cain's death anywhere in the Bible.

Cain argues that the punishment is too great for him to bear, that all those he encounters will try to kill him for what he has done. In response,

God "put a mark on Cain, lest anyone who met him should kill him" (Gen. 4:15). The text doesn't describe the nature of that mark. But the "mark of Cain," intended as a sign of divine protection, becomes something very different in the eyes of many later commentators.

Cain's behavior is regularly decried as barbaric, even bestial. Some, however, depict him as an *actual* beast, an inhuman monster. The mark of Cain is their proof.

In Genesis Rabbah, Abba Yosi claims that "God made a horn grow out of [Cain's] forehead."

Taking this bodily "mark" imagery further, some interpreters write that the mere sight of Cain's repugnant physical bestiality instilled in animals and human beings alike the experience of fear and trembling—and, at times, the powerful impulse to kill.

In Midrash Tanhuma, we are told that as Cain went forth into the world, "wherever he walked, the earth quaked beneath him, and all animals, wild and tame, shaken at the sight of him said, 'What sort of creature is this? . . . Let's go at him and devour him.'"

Later in the book, we find a midrash about Lamech, a grandson of Cain's. It is a strange and disturbing tale that involves a double killing:

> Lamech, seventh in the generations of mankind, who was Cain's grandson, was blind. One time he went out hunting, with his young son holding him by the hand. The child saw something that looked like a beast's horn and said, "I see something that looks like a beast." Lamech bent his bow, [released the arrow], and slew Cain. When the child, still at a distance, saw that it was a dead man with a horn on his forehead, he said to Lamech, "My father, this looks like a slain man with a horn on his forehead." Lamech then cried out, "Woe is me! It is my grandfather!" In contrition, he clapped his two hands together, inadvertently striking the child's head and killing him.

While neither Lamech (who is blind) nor his son (who is far away from the target) knows the true identity of what will become their victim, they kill it anyway. Just the sight of the horned creature elicits an impulse toward murder. That impulse turns tragic. Lamech does much more than kill his grandfather—he breaks God's eternal order of protection. And then, in a wild expression of grief, Lamech accidentally kills his son, too, literally with own hands. Neither deed may be intentional, but the irresistible desire to kill the creature seems to feed on itself and lead to even more killing, from one generation to the next. Everything surrounding Cain results in violence and death.

If Cain is a physically grotesque monster, can he also be a morally wicked person? The "serpent seed" tradition argues that yes, he can be and he is both. While not in accord with the text or the mainstream view, there are works of commentary and imagination (e.g., some of the Gnostic gospels, Pirke de Rabbi Eliezer, parts of the Zohar) that depict Cain as the product of an unholy union between Eve and the serpent, or Satan. In this tradition, Cain is seen as a biological beast *as well as* evil incarnate.

With this backdrop of religious writing about Cain, it should not be much of a surprise that most references to and representations of Cain in secular literature and art are invariably negative and dark. The epic poem *Beowulf*, widely considered the oldest surviving significant work of literature written in English, is a compelling illustration.

At the beginning of the famous legend, the Danes are being ravaged by Grendel, a fierce, bloodthirsty monster. Enraged by the sounds of celebration and joy that emanate from Heorot hall, Grendel menaces the countryside and slaughters scores of innocents:

So times were pleasant for the people there
until finally one, a fiend out of hell,
began to work his evil in the world.
Grendel was the name of this grim demon
haunting the marches, marauding round the heath
and the desolate fens; he had dwelt for a time
in misery among the banished monsters,
Cain's clan, whom the Creator had outlawed
and condemned as outcasts. For the killing of Abel
the Eternal Lord had exacted a price:
Cain got no good from committing that murder
because the Almighty made him anathema

and out of the curse of his exile there sprang
ogres and elves and evil phantoms
and the giants too who strove with God
time and again until He gave them their reward.

According to the narrative, which was composed toward the end of
the first millennium (and translated above by the poet Seamus Heaney),
Grendel is a direct descendent of Cain himself, a "fiend out of hell." Prior
to the start of Grendel's rampage, we are told that he lived among other
monsters who themselves were members of "Cain's clan." These "ogres and
elves and evil phantoms" were outcasts and outlaws, banished from human
civilization and condemned by the same divine curse as their ancestor.

More than a thousand years after the canonization of the Hebrew Bible,
Cain is viewed in this elegiac story as the progenitor, not only of wickedness, but also of the demonic creatures that haunt our minds and imaginations. While Cain's crime and his response to God may have been
expressions of a rebellious, even troubled soul, in *Beowulf* Cain has mutated
into something much more than a rebel or even a sociopath. The references to the birth and existence of other satanic monsters come directly
from the serpent seed tradition. As in the midrash about Lamech, Cain's
killing of Abel and his denial of responsibility will lead to more depravity, more violence, and more death.

Cain's seminal deed and the eternal curse that follows it span the gen-
erations. After Beowulf, a mighty Geat warrior, finally defeats Grendel, he
must still contend with Grendel's mother, a "monstrous hell-bride" who
had been "forced down into fearful waters, / the cold depths, after Cain
had killed / his father's son, felled his own / brother with a sword." Like
the multiheaded hydra of Greek mythology, Cain, his bestial progeny, and
the violent death that always accompanies them never seem to fully die.

While representations of Cain in literature and art seem to "soften" a bit
after the Middle Ages, they are still overwhelmingly hostile. The Renaissance artist Titian (1485–1576), leader of the highly influential sixteenth-
century Venetian school of painting, is a case in point. Titian is widely
regarded as one of the key figures in the history of Western art, and one

of his most imitated works, *Death of Abel*, depicts Cain in an almost bestial way. Pinning his younger brother to a rock with his muscular left leg, a bearded, ferocious-looking Cain raises a huge club above his shoulders. He is about to smash it into Abel, shown writhing on the ground, blood pouring from his head.

Cain is not pictured as a monster, but rather as a human brute who is behaving in a monstrous way. The brothers' bodies are entwined in a frenzy of violence and emotion. There is a flaming altar behind them and nearby, its dark smoke billowing into the sky and serving as a backdrop to Cain's barbaric deed. Is this the smoke from Cain's rejected sacrifice? It isn't clear from the painting. What is clear is Cain's brutality. Titian creates a vivid and chilling portrait of the first murderer and first murder victim.

As a consequence of this primeval event, Cain also becomes history's first outcast. Yet the standard interpretation of his question "Am I my brother's keeper?" makes Cain guilty of a multiplicity of crimes. His punishment is exile and banishment, but for what? Cain murders his brother. He lies to God. And he defies, rejects, or denies the ideas of moral authority and personal responsibility. Which is worse?

With time, artists and writers appear to focus less on Cain's physical violence than on his emotional betrayal of Abel. Marc Chagall (1887–1985) portrays the infamous episode in a very different way from Titian. In *Cain and Abel*, Chagall seems far more intent on evoking contemplation than on eliciting shock. In the lithograph, Cain stands above his brother, his body bent and his right arm outstretched, as if in reluctance or hesitation. In his other hand he holds a small knife, or a dagger. He doesn't wield an enormous club, nor does blood course out of Abel's skull. Instead, Cain aims the blade directly at his brother's chest. It isn't clear if it has penetrated his body yet.

The symbolism of betrayal is profound. Cain has not only failed to serve as the *shomer* of his younger brother; he has "stabbed" him in the heart. Is Chagall suggesting a literal or a figurative murder—the result, it appears, of jealousy and sibling rivalry? Is he planting a seed of sympathy for Cain, depicting him not as a sociopath or a monster, but as a man who has lost control? In Chagall's work, Cain is portrayed as a betrayer and a killer, but he also seems to be depicted as an all-too-human man who has become unhinged by envy, rage, and (perhaps) his *own* perceived betrayal by God.

There are moments in our lives when it is pretty hard to love our neighbors as ourselves—and it is especially challenging when it comes to family members such as siblings. Interpersonal relationships are complex and ever-evolving. Despite our best efforts, favoritism, jealousy, rejection, shame, and enmity can enter the relational dynamic and wreak havoc among even intimate connections. As human beings, we are composites of head and heart; all of us experience (and some of us fall prey to) emotions and impulses. At times, the result can be violent and catastrophic.

Using Cain as the archetype of "public enemy number one," normative religion makes it very clear that we are—that we *must* be—responsible for one another. Unless we want to live in a world of murderers and monsters, what other choice do we have?

BENEFIT OF THE DOUBT

We have seen how perceptions and depictions of Cain have changed over time. In the book of Genesis, Cain kills his brother, Abel, lies to God, and then seems to challenge the necessity (and existence?) of personal responsibility. He is punished with banishment, but he also receives a mark of divine protection. Through the works of later commentators and artists, Cain is transformed from a rebellious sinner into a homicidal sociopath, then a wild animal, and finally an evil, satanic monster.

The message of these interpreters is straightforward: don't violate the moral code, even when no such code has been created, transmitted, or agreed to by others. In this sense, the question "Am I my brother's keeper?" is the height of villainy.

Yet there is another way to interpret Cain's infamous question, *hashomer achi anochi*, one that offers a more sympathetic reading and that gives Cain the benefit of the doubt about his humanity. It is a long-standing (albeit minority) interpretation that preserves the inviolate value and binding nature of our responsibility toward other people and that treats Cain not as a monster, but as a human being. Viewed through this lens, his words are not an outburst of defiance, but an expression of innocent inquiry.

At this early point in the biblical narrative, there is no mention whatsoever of moral rules, social contracts, or divine commandments. Cain and Abel step into a world before civilization, before community, before tribe—a tabula rasa devoid of any organizing principle for interpersonal relationships. When God accepts Abel's offering and rejects Cain's, Cain succumbs to his base drives and kills his younger brother.

After God questions him about Abel's location, Cain utters his three-word response. Which raises a question about his question: is "Am I my brother's keeper?" rhetorical and sarcastic, or does it come from a place that is genuine and heartfelt?

A number of commentators (as well as modern writers and artists) have advocated for the latter interpretation. I noted earlier in the chapter how the placement of the first Hebrew word (*shomer*) is significant. But so is the placement of the final word, *anochi* (I). If Cain's emphasis, or perhaps even his inflection, was on this last word, than a better translation of his question might be, "Am *I* my brother's keeper?"

Despite the inescapable violence of Cain's act, this reading casts his response to God as a serious, earnest, almost childlike question. Without an inherited or concrete system of rules and obligations, how is Cain supposed to know that he is the "keeper" of his brother? How can he be guilty of a crime (or a sin) when he has no code of conduct (or sacred covenant) to follow? This interpretation of Cain's words doesn't whitewash the fact that he has done something unacceptable in God's eyes, but it does raise the issue of culpability. Should Cain bear the *exclusive* responsibility for Abel's death?

This issue is raised in Midrash Tanhuma. After Abel is killed, God says to Cain, "What have you done?" The text imagines Cain responding to God as follows:

I killed Abel [because] you created the evil inclination in me. But you are the keeper (*hashomer*) of all things [yet] you allowed me to kill him. You are the one who killed him—you who are called "I" (*anochi*). Had you accepted my offering as you did his, I would not have been jealous of him.

This bold interpretation of the biblical scene, using Cain's imaginary voice, clearly implies that God is responsible (or at least co-responsible) for the first slaying in history. It has Cain saying, essentially, "Abel may be my victim, but I am yours."

In an earlier work, Genesis Rabbah, Rabbi Shimon bar Yochai offers interpretive commentary that is just as daring—so much so that he prefaces his interpretation with an unusual, somewhat jarring confession: "It is difficult to say this thing, and the mouth cannot utter it plainly."

He then offers a parable about two gladiators fighting before a king. The king could stop the fight any moment he desires, but he does not wish it to end. Instead, he allows it to play out, and one of the fighters is killed. What is the implication? The king, even in his silence, bears deep culpability for the killing. Rabbi Shimon bar Yochai is discomforted by his own analogy because his words implicate God along with Cain (albeit indirectly, via a story) as a key player and guilty party in Abel's killing— and in the sequence of events leading up to it. His midrash challenges the normative view that Cain bears full and sole responsibility for his brother's death. By extension, it also questions God's role in, and culpability for, the existence of immorality and evil in the world.

What the sage fears is that stating such a view could border on blasphemy. So he gives us a parable instead. If God is co-responsible for the slaying of Abel, why is God not co-responsible for all of the mayhem, wickedness, and death that follow?

In light of these two midrashim, it might make more sense to imagine Cain rephrasing his question to God as "Am I *alone* my brother's keeper— are you not as well?" While God doesn't answer Cain in the text, God does do something that suggests a measure of acceptance of responsibility for Abel's death and Cain's fate: God puts a "sign" (*ot* in Hebrew) on Cain, a symbol of God's eternal protection. Is the mark of Cain an expression of divine guilt? Why would God protect Cain for all eternity if Cain was the embodiment of evil and completely irredeemable? Cain may have failed to protect his brother (from himself), but God does not fail to protect Cain (from other people).

We have shown how many interpreters treat the mark of Cain as something negative, a monstrous disfigurement that evokes terror and incites violence. Yet in its appropriate context, the biblical reference to a mark or a sign implies nothing of the sort; it signifies just the opposite. When the word *ot* appears in the Bible, it often has *positive* associations: the rainbow sign following the Flood that signals God's promise never to repeat the act; the mark on male foreskins that links circumcision with entrance into the Hebrew covenant; the signs and wonders that Moses performs before Pharaoh.

In Genesis Rabbah, Rabbi Judah interprets the *ot* that God puts on Cain as having cosmic significance: "God caused the orb of the sun to shine on his account." In the same commentary, Rabbi Hanin claims that through the *ot*, "God made Cain an example to penitents." This reading gives Cain's life ongoing meaning and purpose—a new chapter after his banishment. Rashi, the great medieval commentator, seems to go even further. He writes that the mark on Cain was one of the Hebrew letters of the Tetragrammaton: "[God] engraved a letter of his name onto [Cain's] forehead." For Rashi, the *ot* is not a grotesque horn, but one of the holiest characters from the holiest word in the Jewish tradition. It may not be a "reward" for Cain's actions, but it is clearly meant to set him apart from other people, to protect him, and to bind him to God.

With modernity, the overwhelmingly negative—and often hostile—portraits of Cain that had been so prevalent in the arts for many centuries start to become more nuanced and sympathetic. Tradition seems to be very clear in suggesting that we are indeed the "keepers" of one another's well-being, but the story of Cain and Abel, and God's problematic role in the dynamics of the narrative, makes the issue of personal responsibility more complex than it may first appear. Abel certainly did not deserve to be killed. But if Cain was not exclusively responsible for that tragic outcome (as several interpreters argue quite compellingly), then what does that mean for the rest of us when we feel wronged, abused, or treated by others in an unfair, possibly unjust way?

Lord Byron (1788–1824), perhaps the lead figure in English Romanticism, published *Cain: A Mystery* in 1821. In this dramatic work, Byron tells the biblical story from the perspective of the eponymous character. Cain refuses to offer a prayer of thanksgiving to God because he views mortality as an unjust collective punishment for the sins of two people—his parents. Why should Cain thank God for the "birthright" of death?

In 1857, the French poet Charles Baudelaire (1821–67) published the important modernist work *Les Fleurs du mal*, which includes the poem "Abel et Cain." In it, the "Race of Cain" represents the downtrodden of the world. Unlike "Cain's clan" in *Beowulf*, they are not depicted as evil monsters, but as long-suffering, noble creatures who have been given an unfair fate by their Creator. The poem's last line urges them to rebel against that higher power: "Race of Cain, mount to the sky / And down to the earth cast God!"

In John Steinbeck's (1902–68) classic American novel *East of Eden* (published in 1952), many of the themes from the Genesis story—the struggle for acceptance and approval, favoritism and rejection, sibling rivalry, shame, guilt—are highlighted through the behavior of several main characters (Charles, Adam, Cal, and Aron). Steinbeck avoids rigid characterizations of good and evil and instead weaves together a plot with a more pliant display and equitable assessment of morality and character. No one in the novel is an unmitigated saint or sinner; everyone warrants our sympathy.

Steinbeck uses the story of Cain and Abel as a springboard for his novel and the actions of some of its major characters—and, in the process, conveys his own more nuanced understanding of their guilt and innocence. Byron and Baudelaire are less ambivalent in their judgment. They clearly view Cain as an innocent, or at least an all-too-human pawn in an unjust and dangerous game. Is there more than one victim in the biblical tale? Is Cain a victim of divine capriciousness as well as of his own ignorance about how to live in civilized society? Who in the story is responsible for whom—and for what? If the border between keeper and criminal is as porous as it seems when the text is read closely, then how are we supposed to know how to live our lives today?

MISTAKES WERE MADE

Depending on how we read it, Cain's "Am I my brother's keeper?" makes him into either a monster or history's first real human being. In its narrative context, the question brings into sharp relief the concept of personal responsibility, but it also suggests many other ideas and tensions: virtue and vice, fate and freedom, victimhood, and God's culpability for (and complicity in) the existence of evil. As with many questions in the Bible, it raises other questions: Is ignorance of the law justification for breaking it? Are moral rules valid only after they are "officially" introduced? What is God's role in the creation of social contracts and civilizations?

We know from popular culture, politics, and everyday life that it is never good enough to simply say that "mistakes were made." In the end, *someone* has to take responsibility in the aftermath of errors and crimes, injustice and violence. That's why, when no one does—or when individuals deny their responsibility—we hold trials and set up congressional hearings, truth commissions, and international tribunals. People and societies need to believe in, and enforce, a moral order. To satisfy our sense of justice. To exact retribution from wrongdoers. To see that wickedness is punished.

Without accountability, human life (to paraphrase Thomas Hobbes in *Leviathan*) would be nasty, brutish, and short. In the absence of rules and regulations to govern our behavior—and structures in place to enforce those rules and protect people from one another—there would be anarchy and mayhem. Rivalry could lead to open and violent conflict. Rejection could fuel homicidal rage. While relativism is an attractive position when applied to certain social and cultural issues, it offers a very unsatisfying intellectual stance when it comes to matters of life and death. Is it *ever* acceptable to intentionally kill an innocent person? Experience tells us that our actions must have consequences for our world to function with a sense of safety. If there is no threat of punishment, how do we deter harmful behavior? A system of morality has to exist. Or it must be created.

For atheists and nontheists, it is human beings who are the architects of moral systems, the rules, laws, and codes that allow societies to function in (reasonably) fair, just, and safe ways. Because our free choices cannot be allowed to run rampant and damage or destroy the freedom of others, most societies and nations choose to govern actions and protect individual liberty with covenants of power and authority. Whether it is the Constitution, the Magna Carta, or other legislative documents, these social contracts serve as the foundation of legal and (many of us believe) ethical behavior, the transactions and interactions between and among people that occur on a daily basis.

For theists, it is God who is the bedrock *beneath* the foundation, the Creator of all things—including morality. How can morality truly exist if it does not emerge from an authoritative source, or a higher power, beyond human decision making or consensus? For conservative religionists and biblical literalists, God is that source, the author of specific rules, regulations, and commandments that tell us what to do and what not to do. For liberal thinkers, God is not the literal author of moral laws but the "muse," or inspiration, behind them. That makes morality the result of a divine-human (or I-Thou, to reference Martin Buber) relationship, and it means that some ethical beliefs and practices will change over time— just as we, and our societies, change and evolve.

The narrative of Cain and Abel underscores these issues and tensions.

It seems an almost inescapable (and inexplicable) fact that when God rejects Cain's offering and accepts the offering of his brother, Abel, God also *victimizes* Cain. Does that make God co-responsible for the lethal chain of events that follows? If God is responsible for goodness, why shouldn't God also be held responsible—in some way, shape, or form— for evil? And if we are free to choose between right and wrong, who other than God gave us that freedom? Was it a gift that was premature, even dangerous?

The answers to these questions about moral responsibility are not simple and clean. Nor is the answer as to how to properly translate and read Cain's words.

Which interpretation of Cain's question—and which version of his personality—is the "correct" one? In my view, there are two Cains: the bestial amoralist *as well as* the questioner and rebel. Any intellectual or literary approach that reduces Cain to a black-or-white caricature (rather than a more complex, yet more genuine, character) ignores centuries of commentary and interpretation. By extension, a more nuanced position about morality itself seems to make the most sense. We can believe in a moral order. We can even believe that God is (directly or indirectly) responsible for it. Neither belief, however, is incompatible with the idea that some moral rules can and do change over time, and that ethical social systems must be reviewed and renewed on a constant basis.

This sensibility makes protest and rebellion not only inevitable, but *necessary* features of human life. Two months after the Constitution was signed, Thomas Jefferson famously argued that rebellion against the status quo should occur every twenty years. Albert Camus (1913–60) claims in *The Rebel* that when human beings experience disenchantment over how justice is applied by those in authority, they should rebel. Rebellion, for Camus, is the product of a basic contradiction between the human mind's ceaseless quest for clear understanding and the (apparently) meaningless nature of the world around us.

He writes, "What is a rebel? A man who says no, but whose refusal does not imply a renunciation. He is also a man who says yes, from the moment he makes his first gesture of rebellion." Why is rebellion an act of affirmation rather than one of renunciation? Because when we reject a problematic status quo, we are, in essence, advocating for a vision of a better state, a new and improved situation. The rebel fights *for* something in the very same breath that he or she fights *against* something else. The rebel's soul isn't rooted in negativity or rage. It is animated by hopefulness and passion.

When we feel oppressed, when authority threatens our autonomy, when "justice" seems capricious, unclear, or unfair, the impulse to protest and rebel is a natural one. Cain is far from a model of saintly virtue, but his reaction to God's unfathomable rejection of his sacrificial gift—shame, despair, confusion, anger, and violence—seems more human than demonic. The biblical story seems to be telling Cain, *Yes, you are your brother's keeper, even if no one informed you prior to your actions.* But the interpretive tradition seems to be telling the rest of us, *No, God did not do enough to prevent this tragedy. In fact, God played an active role in making history's first murder possible at all.*

When many of us look at the world today, rife with injustice and disorder, tragedy and disease, we often wonder whether God made a mistake. Did God give humanity free will too soon? Why do good people suffer?

Are we alone responsible for all of the bad things that occur in life, or are there other forces at work? If human beings are supposed to watch over each other, who is supposed to watch over all human beings?

The (young and inexperienced) God we see depicted in the early chapters of the book of Genesis borders at times on the abusive. In chapter four, God rejects Cain's offering (and Cain himself?) without a word of explanation and then proceeds to curse him when Cain is at his most raw and vulnerable. A few verses later in the narrative, the same God places a mark of eternal protection on Cain in an expression of compassion. God's behavior turns their relationship into an emotional roller coaster. If God is this inconsistent, unpredictable, confusing, and irresponsible toward Cain, how are Cain's descendants—all of us—expected to know how to behave toward one another?

Individual human beings may or may not possess an innate sense of moral duty, but it is something that can develop in us as a result of our ethical behavior. The doing of good can often produce the feeling of *wanting* to do good. Whether it is showing empathy toward a brother or, as I described at the start of this chapter, trying to offer solace to a congregant and his family in the face of a terminal illness, our interactions with others largely define who we are—and they often transform us, giving us a feeling of purpose and value. I am a better rabbi for having known and cared for a family in distress. I am worse for having removed myself from that world of moral possibilities.

My awareness of that disconnect helps to guide me as I strive to discern the next chapter of my career.

4

Mission (Im)Possible

I GRADUATED FROM COLLEGE WITH a degree in philosophy and no plan for my future. In the months prior to graduation, I'd explored the possibility of pursuing either a PhD in metaphysics or, instead, an MFA in creative writing. I was attracted to the (somewhat naïve) idea that an academic career would provide the most likely context in which I could cultivate a life of the mind. As a young poet and writer, I was also drawn to the (overly romantic) idea of entering a formal writing program, which I thought would allow me to gain entry into the rarefied world of books and letters.

In the end, I rejected both options. A life in academia seemed too detached from the real world and getting an MFA before I'd experienced much more of life struck me as a bit ludicrous. I craved something more active, more *adventurous.*

I decided to move to Cambridge, Massachusetts, to write the Great American Novel. I'd written a novella in college and I wanted to give myself the time, and the focus, to develop it into a larger narrative. I could have moved anywhere, in theory, but two of my closest friends were moving to Cambridge as well: Arjun, an Indian American who was beginning a PhD program in Sanskrit at Harvard, and Steven, a Jesuit priest who was studying for his licentiate degree at the Weston School of Theology. I met Arjun in college and Steven during my junior year abroad in Jerusalem.

While I spent most days working on my novel, I spent many evenings and late nights with Arjun and Steven. It was during those scotch-infused encounters that I continued my exploration of metaphysics, a subject I'd been interested in since I was very young. At the age of three, I had a serious heart procedure, a surgery and early trauma that in many ways led to my asking the Big Questions throughout my life: *Is death the end? What is the purpose of life? Does God exist?* The three of us—a Catholic priest, a Hindu graduate student, and a Jewish writer—discussed and debated these and other questions with great enthusiasm, and I loved every minute of it.

As a result, in part, of our conversations on spirituality, theology, and the nature of existence, I thought it was critical for me as a Jew to read the Torah in its entirety for the first time. I wanted to study its tales and teachings, not as a child sitting reluctantly in Hebrew school, but as a willing and intellectually curious adult. Studying in Jerusalem, both at the university and at ultraorthodox yeshivas, had begun to open my mind to the richness and power of sacred texts, but I yearned for more. I chose to focus on the Five Books of Moses because I viewed them as the foundation of my faith.

One evening, after an especially animated and rewarding debate about God, revelation, and the description of the theophany at Mount Sinai in the book of Exodus, Steven asked me if I'd ever thought about entering the rabbinate.

"Are you kidding me?" I responded. "Me—a *rabbi*? No, never!"

"It's just that you're so impassioned and engaged by God and religion," he said. "That's a vocation where you could devote your life to both of them."

"I am passionate about those subjects. But I raised hell in college—I drank like a fish and I slept around. I spent a night in jail last summer for destroying property at a nightclub. I've got lots of inner demons. I'm not worthy."

"*None* of us are worthy. What matters is whether you're called."

Steven's words caught me off guard. Here was my friend the priest—my tranquil, righteous, celibate friend—telling a restless seeker and libertine like myself that a career path I'd never even considered possible was open to me. I'd always felt that I was too imperfect, too deeply "human" to serve others—let alone lead them.

"Do me a favor," Steven went on. "Read First Samuel, chapter three. The opening verses of the book. Then let me know what you think."

I read the verses when I got back to my apartment. They tell the story of Samuel's prophetic call. God calls to the young Samuel three times, and each time, Samuel mistakes the divine call for the voice of his master, Eli. It is only when God calls to him a fourth time that he finally recognizes God and responds, "Here I am."

I understood Steven's message. And something in my soul resonated with those verses from First Samuel. I didn't know whether my heart surgery had been the cause or simply the catalyst for my quest for spiritual knowledge, but my wish to find answers to the big questions—as I came to discern through the help of my Jesuit friend—was, below the surface, actually a desire to connect with God in a direct and personal way.

Was God calling me, or was I calling God?

Within days, I'd ordered course catalogs from the three major nonorthodox rabbinical schools (I knew I would never fit into the traditionalist Jewish world). I read their lists of courses—Bible, theology, Talmud, liturgy, midrash. I imagined devoting five years of my life to studying sacred texts, and it felt right. I started to think about religion—Judaism, in my case—as the concretization of metaphysical ideas. I saw its rites, rituals, and ceremonies as tactile expressions of spiritual realities. For me, philosophy and literature could only go so far as conduits to the sacred. Religion, by its very nature, was a response to transcendence. And it was more direct, overt, and transformative.

I was accepted to rabbinical school and I chose to enroll in the Reform movement's seminary, Hebrew Union College–Jewish Institute of Religion. When I finished my book and my year in Cambridge came to an end, I said goodbye to Steven and Arjun and traveled to Sitka, Alaska, to attend a writers' symposium and workshop my novel. A month later, I packed my bags and flew to Jerusalem to begin my studies.

Today, twenty-five years since those experiences, I often wonder whether I still hear the call. There are times when I think I do, such as when I as a visitor hear a mediocre sermon and want to leap out of the pew and deliver a better one from the pulpit myself. And there are times when I most decidedly do not, like when I hear another horror story about a rabbinic colleague whose contract wasn't renewed by his or her board, or who has simply burned out. I am less naive now about life and about the reality of being a contemporary rabbi. Yet the coal still smolders. And I am no less hungry.

"What does the Lord *your God demand of you?"*
(Deuteronomy 10:12)

By the tenth chapter in the book of Deuteronomy, the Israelites have reached a pivotal stage in their journey from slavery in Egypt to hope in the Promised Land. For the first time in many years, the people of Israel will be exposed to foreign cultures and alien religious practices and ideas. Since their own monotheistic religion is still in a nebulous and fragile state, the possibility of outside influence, particularly idolatry, is a looming danger and a grave concern. They need clarity, and Moses tries to provide it in the wide-ranging discourses and sets of laws in this chapter and the others around it.

Moses is at a pivotal point in his journey as well: he is near the end of his life. When he is gone, the Israelites will be in need of strong guidance. As their current leader, Moses makes the judgment that what his people will need is not just clarity about their religious practice, but clarity about their existential *purpose*. So he asks them,

> And now, O Israel, what does the Lord your God demand of you? Only this: to fear the Lord your God, to walk only in His paths, to love Him, and to serve the Lord your God with all your heart and soul, keeping the Lord's commandments and laws, which I enjoin upon you today, for your good. (Deut. 10:12–13)

Moses's question is profoundly teleological. And because he proffers an answer in the same verse, it is also rhetorical and pedagogic. What is the purpose of the lives of the people of Israel—and, by extension, the lives of all those generations that follow?

Understood more broadly, what is our "mission" as human beings?

The answer to this seemingly straightforward question is not a simple one. In fact, it is not even clear from the structure of the text whether the response to the question is a single "answer," an answer with subcategories, or multiple and coequal answers.

In my view, there are five separate and distinct (yet interrelated) components to the response, and they appear in the following order after Moses's initial, all-encompassing, teleological question, "What does the LORD your God demand of you?":

1. Fear God.
2. Walk in God's paths.
3. Love God.
4. Serve God with heart and soul.
5. Keep God's commandments and laws.

If we group all five of these elements together into a single answer, we are left with a response so general and vague that it is functionally useless. Do all five attitudes and actions have the same value? Must we feel or perform each one at the same time—and, if so, how is that possible? What, if any, relationship exists between them?

Another response is to treat the first "requirement" as the primary answer to the question, and to view the others as its subcategories, or secondary (and explanatory) answers. With the fear of God at the top of the list, this approach creates a sense of hierarchy and supports the need for prioritization: If we start by keeping the commandments, we can progress up the spiritual ladder to the more important and meritorious experience of fear, or *yirah*.

A third way of interpreting the response is to read all five requirements as independent yet interrelated and coequal parts of the same answer. Rather than viewing the different components as variations on a theme or secondary explanations, this approach treats each one as a discrete obligation; while every one of them is necessary to fulfill our sacred mission, none of them is sufficient in and of itself. There may be no hierarchy or particular order by which we must observe the requirements, but together they constitute a pathway that is multivalent and indivisible.

Moses's question and the responses that follow generate multiple interpretations and great ambiguity. And if we can't fully understand what exactly his words mean, then how can we possibly fulfill our mandate as human beings? Has the Torah presented us with a "mission impossible" or a roadmap for more purposeful lives?

In order of appearance, the first thing that Moses highlights in response to his question about what God wants from us is *yirah*, the fear of God: "What does the LORD your God demand of you? Only this: to fear the LORD your God." The verse continues, but the fact that the conjunction *ki im* (usually translated as "only" or "but") precedes the word *yirah* rather than the words and requirements that follow it is noteworthy. Does *ki im* connote accessibility, as in *merely* to fear God (along with other obligations), or exclusivity, as in *solely* to fear God (which excludes, or subsumes, the other four duties)?

Rabbi Levi Yitzhak of Berditchev (1740–1809), a highly influential leader of the early Hasidic movement, favors the former interpretation. He teaches that the fear of God was a "small matter" for the Israelites in biblical times, since they had personally witnessed God's miracles and marvels; that is why, for him, *ki im* should be read as "merely." In a story in *Al ha-Torah* about the Hasidic master, Levi Yitzhak is shown challenging God when God questions his people's faith and devotion: "Give my generation the likes of the Exodus and see how for us, too, the fear of God will be a 'small matter!'"

In contrast, the Babylonian Talmud favors the latter interpretation, which treats *yirah* as a singular and uniquely significant commandment: "Everything is in the hands of heaven except [humanity's] fear of heaven" (BT Berachot 33b). It is the fear of God *alone*, among all that inheres in the world (including the other commandments), over which God does not have any control. God asks for fear "only," not "merely"; rather than being a small matter, *yirah* is exceptional, a mind-set/feeling/duty that is qualitatively different from and greater than all others, and that is realizable only through human effort. Does divine fear stand separate and apart from other obligations, or is it linked to them? The uniqueness and gravitas of *yirah* make it difficult to answer.

Regardless of whether *yirah* is the "first among equals" or the primary and catchall concept for the obligations that follow, its placement at the very beginning of Moses's response suggests that it is of enormous import. But why is the fear of God so essential to living lives of purpose and meaning, lives that involve a deep and intimate relationship with the divine? Is *yirah* an emotion, an attitude, an activity, or an experience? Is it connected to inner spirituality, moral behavior, or both?

There is no single and universally agreed-on definition of *yirah*, just as there is no single way to interpret Moses's multidimensional answer.

The fear of God has been a fundamental motif in Judaism for nearly three millennia. While its role in the religious life reached more colorful and pronounced expression in esoteric circles, the concept was never absent from the normative tradition. The person who possessed the "fear of God" was depicted as a model Jew, someone of deep faith and high ethical principles. The idea, however, remained relatively amorphous for many centuries; it seemed to designate certain *general* religious qualities, but its precise meaning was never systematically explored until the Middle Ages.

Yirah as a religious notion has roots as far back as the book of Genesis. In the story of the binding of Isaac, Abraham is called a *yerei Elohim*, or "fearer of God" (Gen. 22:12). In this context, as Kierkegaard explains at length in *Fear and Trembling*, *yirah* seems to have more to do with faith and submission than it does with morality and righteous behavior. Still, as many other theologians observe, the fear of God also seems to express an especially profound and intense relationship with God, particularly as realized in terms of a person's ethical conduct. Job, for instance, is described as "blameless and upright; he feared God and shunned evil" (Job 1:1).

The Bible suggests elsewhere (in Ps. 112:1 and Prov. 19:23) that the fear of God is necessary for a life of happiness and virtue. The concept of *yirah* is also connected to specific interpersonal relations (described in chapters 19 and 25 of the book of Leviticus). The fear of God finds yet another association with regard to maturity and the life of the mind, as in "The beginning of wisdom is the fear of the LORD" (Ps. 111:10) and "The fear of the LORD is the beginning of knowledge" (Prov. 1:7).

In rabbinic literature, the fear of God is generally called *yirat shamayim* (as opposed to *yirat Elohim* or *yirat Adonai*), yet its exact meaning remains unclear. In this genre, the fear of God is often linked to the love of God, and discussions on the topic tend to focus on the interrelationship between these two attitudes/responses to God. (The requirement to "love God" is the third aspect of Moses's answer to the question about life's purpose, and I will explore it later in the chapter.)

In medieval thought, religious fear is subdivided into two discrete types: the fear of punishment (*yirat ha-onesh*) and fear of God's majesty (*yirat ha-rommemut*). In his influential work *The Book of Principles*, Rabbi Joseph Albo (1380–1444) writes that the fear of punishment, while not meritorious in itself, is necessary for the attainment of the fear of God's majesty, a much higher and less externally oriented religious quality. The former kind of fear, he comments, may help to restrain and subdue a person's desires and physical nature, but the latter type, better understood as *awe*, is reason's innate response to the revelation of the religious truth embedded within it.

Rabbi Elijah de Vidas (1518–92) challenges this rationalistic view. He devotes the first chapters of his book *The Beginning of Wisdom* to theosophical reflections on fear and sin. In the Kabbalistic context out of which he writes, the fear of punishment (for sin), far from being merely the fear of self-harm and a tool against temptation, becomes instead the fear of causing a "flaw" in the divine cosmos. Though it is not as lofty as the awe brought about by *yirat ha-rommemut*, *yirat ha-onesh* it is not denigrated by de Vidas; it is seen, not as qualitatively different, but as part of the same spectrum.

Prior to the start of the Hasidic period (near the middle of the eighteenth century), discussions on the fear of God generally approached the subject from ethical, pietistic, or philosophical perspectives. While there were some notable exceptions—mostly in mystical circles—it is only after the birth of Hasidism that a sophisticated and well-developed *phenomenological* exploration of *yirah* emerges. Though they ground themselves in the Kabbalistic hermeneutics and ideas that form their intellectual inheritance, the Hasidic mystics move beyond theosophical speculation and examine the fear of God as it relates to *devekut*—the raw encounter with divine reality.

In chapter two, I highlighted an example of the role of fear in early Hasidic thought through the writings of Rabbi Dov Baer of Mezeritch, the Great Maggid. For him, *yirah* is associated with—and an effect of—the experience of divine-human encounter, a metaphysical collision through which a person's capacities and sense of self are wiped out while in the awe-inspiring presence of God. Yet that experience of awe can also lead to primal terror. The Maggid writes that at the moment of *devekut*, a "fire of silence" descends on the mystic and a "great fear" grips that person's soul. As a result, the mystic loses all orientation and enters a transformative state of ecstasy.

There are many different categories and definitions of *yirah*: fear, awe, terror, even reverence, to name just a few. So when we are told by Moses to "fear God" in Deuteronomy 10:12, which sort of *yirah* is it that we are being asked to demonstrate and/or experience? Does it relate to morality, spirituality, or philosophical insight?

Viewed through the lens of religious thought, the answer is not at all clear. But poets and writers have tried to dive into the murky waters of the topic as well.

In his poem "The Tyger," William Blake (1757–1827) captures several of the meanings and nuances of *yirah*, and he does it in a deceptively simple, almost childlike way:

Tyger Tyger burning bright,
In the forests of the night:
What immortal hand or eye,
Dare frame thy fearful symmetry?

How does the experience of watching a wild animal relate to God? For Blake, the mere *fact* of such a mysterious and terrifying creature is inspirational. Its existence also raises a question: who, or what, possesses the imagination and ability to create such a seemingly otherworldly being? In this respect, the tiger is revelatory, a living testament to its Creator, a trace of the transcendent force that formed it. Rather than a work of art, it is a mark of divinity. When we, like Blake, tremble in the presence of such a majestic creature, that fear is merely a mask for our awe of, and reverence for, God.

C. S. Lewis (1898–1963) references the concept of the fear of God in many of his writings, but he describes it in a specific way in his book *The Problem of Pain*. Lewis writes that when one experiences the fear of the numinous (a word coined by the German theologian Rudolf Otto to denote divine reality), it is not a feeling akin to the fear that one feels in the presence of a tiger, or even a ghost. Instead, the fear of the numinous instills in a person a sensation of awe, a feeling that produces "wonder and a certain shrinking." A brush with transcendence enthralls and humbles us, and it seizes our entire being. While it may not be a rational experience, it is a *relational* one; the encounter with the divine compels us to take a step back, recalibrate where we stand, and reassess who we are.

Fear, awe, and reverence are rooted in more than pure emotion. Maimonides writes in the *Mishneh Torah* that when one reflects on the world in its totality, with its vast web of living beings and natural phenomena, one immediately "trembles and grows fearful, for he becomes aware that he is a tiny and lowly creature, with meager knowledge compared to Him who possesses perfect knowledge." When we try to fathom our existential reality, our finitude in relation to the Creator's infinity, we will inevitably experience responses that make us "fearful." Yet that fear can serve as a gateway, helping to break down our defenses and opening our souls to the presence of the transcendent.

God requires that we do—and that we be—several things, but striving to become "fearers of God" is first and foremost among them. Although it is not completely clear whether *yirah* is connected to morality, spirituality, or reflection, the possession and expression of the fear of God seems to be a prerequisite for living a godly and purpose-driven life. It also seems to be linked with humility, an internal quality with external reach, something that is felt in the soul but that is demonstrated through word and deed.

The great American poet Robert Frost (1874–1963) tries to express this idea through his poem "The Fear of God," which he wrote in the latter years of his life and long after he had achieved enormous fame, even celebrity, for his work:

If you should rise from Nowhere up to Somewhere,
From being No one up to being Someone,

Be sure to keep repeating to yourself
You owe it to an arbitrary god
Whose mercy to you rather than to others
Won't bear to critical examination.
Stay unassuming. If for lack of license
To wear the uniform of who you are,
You should be tempted to make up for it
In a subordinating look or toe,
Beware of coming too much to the surface
And using for apparel that was meant
To be the curtain of the inmost soul.

Frost seems to be addressing himself as well as any of us who has "risen" from obscurity to renown, from "nowhere" to "somewhere." Rather than allowing that experience to lead to arrogance or a sense of entitlement, Frost implies that the fear of God will help us to stay humble and unassuming—and aware that randomness and luck, not necessarily merit, played a key role in our success. By keeping ourselves grounded and "low" (as described in chapter 2), we will avoid the dangers of "coming too much to the surface," of thinking that we are anything other than human and imperfect.

For Frost, the fear of God is more about insight and perspective than ethics or spirituality. Yet they are involved, too. Instead of treating fame (or achievement, power, influence, wealth) as a cloak with which to adorn ourselves, we should view it as a "curtain" that, when opened, discloses our characters, passions, dreams, and souls.

What is the mission of human beings? To never to lose sight of our humanity.

AT THE THRESHOLD

It is beyond the scope of this chapter to explore all five components of the answer to the question in Deuteronomy 10:12: "And now, O Israel, what does the LORD your God demand of you?" Each one easily warrants a book in and of itself. My focus on *yirah* is both pedagogic (I favor the talmudic view on the concept's uniqueness and power) and personal (*yirah* was the subject of my rabbinic thesis and first book, *Forests of the Night: The Fear of God in Early Hasidic Thought*).

The fear of God is a concept with many and varied interpretations: Is it connected to attitude, action, or experience? Does it relate to morality, spirituality, or philosophical thought? The answers are not at all clear. Yet *yirah* is only *one* of the five different elements that together constitute the response to the question. Even if we fully understood the meaning of each and every element, the task would appear daunting. Since the meaning(s) is(are) not certain, how can we reasonably be asked to take on, let alone complete, our "mission"?

Rabbi Joseph Albo, whom I cited earlier in this chapter, does not think that the response is confusing or the task formidable. But in order to proceed properly, he argues, we must first understand the aim of the question, the end goal, the purpose of life. He writes in *The Book of Principles*,

> The objective which the soul is capable of attaining while in the body by performing the commandments of the Torah is nothing else than the permanent acquisition of a disposition to fear God. And when it acquires this attribute of fearing God, the soul is elevated and is prepared to attain eternal life. . . . Hence the expression in the Torah "You shall fear the Lord your God" (Deut. 6:13), while a specific command, is [also] a general principle, embracing all the commandments of the Torah, or a great many of them. For fear is that state of mind which is acquired through the commandments of the Torah, and it is the noblest disposition for a man to acquire.

The goal and purpose of human life is to elevate the soul and prepare it for eternal life. For that to occur, we must acquire the permanent disposition, or mind-set, to fear God. As a specific command as well as a general principle, the fear of God embraces most of the other commandments in the Torah—yet it is also acquired *through* them. How does Albo make sense of this apparent paradox? He continues,

> In order to attain the perfection of one's soul, a person should fear God, walk in God's ways, love God, and serve God with all his heart

and soul. But it is exceptionally difficult for a person to attain the required degree of fear, love, and service with all his heart and soul. Hence God made it easier for man. God commanded him instead to observe merely God's statutes and commandments, thereby achieving the same degree of perfection he would get from service with [full] heart and soul.

After highlighting the other four elements in the response to this chapter's question, Albo notes the extreme difficulty that human beings face when we try to realize them with all our "heart and soul." This important qualification makes it plain that perfunctory adherence to, or near-attainment of, these qualities is not sufficient. Whether it is the requirement of fear (*yirah*), love (*ahavah*), or service (*avodah*), a radical commitment of one's heart and soul must be present to fulfill the divine charge.

That's the seemingly insurmountable challenge. Yet Albo writes that God makes it "easier" for humanity to achieve self-perfection by treating the entirety of the ritual and ethical obligations of the Torah as a kind of *surrogate* for the spiritual qualities themselves. Through the mediation of the commandments, the formidability of the task is mitigated, if not neutralized. We "merely" (*ki im*, as discussed previously) need to observe God's laws and precepts in order to uplift and transform our souls.

Having explained *how* it is possible for human beings to realize the highest degrees of spiritual perfection (despite their apparent remoteness), Albo then explains *why* it is essential that we strive for them with such dogged resolve:

What does God ask of you? Instead of the fear of God, instead of walking in God's ways and loving God, instead of serving God with all your heart and soul, all of which you are obliged to do— God asks you merely to keep the divine commandments and statutes "which I enjoin upon you today, for your good," i.e., all this is for your [own] good, because by keeping the commandments of the Torah one may come to realize the purpose of human life [which would otherwise be attained only] through great labor and enormous effort.

In an act of divine compassion, God allows the system of command-ments to function as the intermediary between humanity and the most exalted of spiritual qualities, which reach their apex in the fear of God. And since God would never require us to do anything that wasn't possible in principle, all of the qualities are accessible to us, even if we have to take an indirect route to experience or achieve them. Further, they are *for our own good*, that is, they offer us a means to realize our raison d'être as humans.

This is a very different view from that of Maimonides, who describes a path to the fear of God that is highly contemplative and analytical (and likely accessible only to an elite, educated demographic). Instead, Albo's path is pragmatic (and more democratic), substituting the practice of deeds and the performance of rituals for direct metaphysical knowledge. The fear of God is still the ultimate objective and the goal of human life, but the way we reach/realize/experience it is far more accessible.

Soul elevation and self-perfection are, in Albo's thought, intimately linked with the fear of God; taken together, the actualization of this tri-umvirate of qualities constitutes the existential mission of human beings and the path by which we are able to prepare for the world-to-come. Yet the notion of viewing life's teleological work as preparation for *eternal* life predates Albo by at least a millennium. In *Pirke Avot* we find the fol-lowing teaching: "Rabbi Jacob said: This world is like an antechamber (*prozdor*) before the world-to-come. Prepare yourself in the antecham-ber, so that you can enter the great hall" (*Avot* 4:21).

What does the LORD *your God demand of you?* This mishnaic text, through an artful use of metaphor, suggests that our purpose in life is nothing less—and nothing more—than to prepare ourselves (our souls?) for the world-to-come. The Greek word *prozdor* can be translated in many ways: antechamber, corridor, passageway. For many commentators, the image represents the totality of mortal existence. Rashi expands the imag-ery and interprets the teaching in an anthropomorphic way: life is the entry hall, or threshold space, that leads to the king.

According to Rashi, the sole focus of our thoughts during our lifetimes should be on that inevitable, anxiety-producing, and exhilarating encoun-ter. What would ordinary people do while they were waiting to meet and impress a flesh-and-blood ruler? They would straighten their clothes, fix their hair, get ready to present themselves as best they could. For Rashi, our lives must similarly be spent in preparation for and anticipation of the meeting with the "king of kings"—not through fancy attire or personal grooming, but through inner attitude and outer action.

The text from *Pirke Avot* continues, "[Rabbi Jacob] would say: Better is one hour of repentance and good deeds in this world than the entirety of life [eternal] in the world-to-come. Better is one hour of blissfulness of spirit in the world-to-come than the entirety of a lifetime spent in this world" (*Avot* 4:22).

While the first part of Rabbi Jacob's teaching describes life as an "antechamber" and contrasts it with to the world-to-come, the second part offers paradoxical observations about the two realities. Initially, Rabbi Jacob tells us to live our lives in preparation for a (greater) life with God. But then he states that our penitent souls and good deeds in this world, even if they only last "one hour," are superior to eternal life itself. In the very next line, however, Rabbi Jacob seems to say exactly the opposite: just one hour of "blissfulness of spirit" in the world-to-come will supersede (in worth and sense of satisfaction) any and all activity in life.

Are spiritual disposition and righteous behavior ends in themselves, or are they means to an end? Some commentators argue that, though bound by time and mortality, repentance and good deeds can afford us a *taste* of heaven while we are still alive on the earth. Rabbi Jacob, however, is silent on the matter, apparently content to let future generations debate—and wrestle with—the paradox.

There is another paradox involved in this teaching: the very same threshold (*prozdor*) that leads to God also *separates* us from God. The goal of our lives, it seems, is to work to bridge or collapse that distance. Life is liminality, a place of transition and constant flux. The image of a *prozdor* is an especially apt one. On one level, mortal existence is a kind of "waiting room," a place to ponder and prepare before the "great meeting" that awaits us all. On another level, we can encounter *godliness* in life itself, through inner work and moral action. If the purpose of our lives is to strive for closeness with God, this tension will be ever present.

A *prozdor* is a compelling symbol. It represents a transition from one space, or one reality, to another. A threshold can remind us of what we must leave behind, but it can also serve as the gateway to future promise. As T. S. Eliot (1888–1965) writes in "Little Gidding," one of his last major poems,

> What we call the beginning is often the end
> And to make an end is to make a beginning.
> The end is where we start from.

In its best manifestation, a *prozdor* represents hope, opportunity, possibility. Yet it can also be the cause of intense anxiety, even a sense of dread. When we stand at a threshold, we often feel as if we are neither here nor there: we teeter in liminal space, unsure of our footing and uncertain about our next steps. A threshold can usher in change, but it can also trigger feelings of panic.

Rabbi Gil Steinlauf writes in a sermon that it is "no wonder that we Jews put mezuzahs on our doorways to this day with the words of the Sh'ma, words of affirmation, tradition, and comfort, to accompany us as we transition from one place to another in life." As we cross the threshold and move from one physical space to another throughout the day—or from one existential place to another during our lives—the symbol and substance of the mezuzah offers us a sense of security, and it has for many centuries.

The world, and the totality of existence, is a *prozdor*, a threshold before and a gateway to the world-to-come. Yet because we can experience a taste of heaven in the here and now, human life is fundamentally about *doing*, not just *waiting*. Or, as Steinlauf puts it, the meaning of the passage from *Pirke Avot* is "not that all the good stuff is in heaven after you die. It's a deeper wisdom teaching: that we must first understand that everything about our life, our world is transitional and transitory. Understand that, and that is the beginning of True Wisdom."

Which brings us back to a central motif in this chapter: "The beginning of wisdom is the fear of the LORD" (Ps. 111:10).

Even in the face of liminality, even when we are anxious or fearful, our actions are still necessary, and in some ways almost involuntary. To be human is to seek, to yearn, to explore. Eliot goes on in his poem,

We shall not cease from exploration
And the end of all our exploring
Will be to arrive where we started
And know the place for the first time.
Through the unknown, remembered gate
When the last of earth left to discover
Is that which was the beginning.

Living at the threshold—living at all, really—means that our perceptions of time and self will always be in a state of flux: ends will give birth to new beginnings, and beginnings will eventually transform into ends. We have little choice but to embark, and embark again and again, on the ever-cyclical journey. Yet our souls crave rest. And completion. When our exploration comes to a close, our focus will shift from perception to *recognition*. We will see, and we will be wise enough to finally understand, that the end we longed for was actually just another beginning.

There is a story, drawn from *Tales of the Hasidim*, about Rabbi Shlomo of Karlin (1740–92) that illustrates the phenomenon of human longing:

Once, at the close of the Day of Atonement, when Rabbi Shlomo was in an affable mood, he announced that he would tell anyone who inquired what it was that that person had asked of God during the holy days, as well as what the response would be. To the first of his disciples who wanted to be told, [Rabbi Shlomo] said: "What you asked of God was that God should give you your livelihood at the proper time and without travail, so that you might not be hindered in serving God. And the answer is that what God really wants of you is not study or prayer, but the sighs of your heart, which is [now] breaking because the travail of gaining a livelihood hinders you in the service of God."

The disciple in this story yearns for both an end and a beginning: He wants an end to his worries about making a living and the start of an unencumbered, uninterrupted connection to God through sacred service. The necessities and challenges of basic human existence (e.g., earning an income and paying bills) probably seem intolerable to this student and seeker. How can he stand at the threshold, in the *prozdor*, when he is aware of what awaits him on the other side?

The rabbi informs the disciple that his prayer will not be answered. He must work like everyone else; he must struggle and toil through the "passageway" of life even if it means he will not be able to devote his efforts exclusively and without distraction to spiritual pursuits. *What does the* LORD *your God demand of you?* God wants the disciple's "sighs of the heart," his imperfect efforts, his striving, his travail. What God truly desires is not "study or prayer," but longing *itself*.

When we crave something, we tolerate the discomfort of our pangs in the hope that they will one day be satiated.

When we yearn, when our soul aches to be united with another, we put ourselves in a place of vulnerability and risk.

Is there any better way to show our devotion or our love?

HEAVEN AND EARTH

Mortal existence is a *prozdor*, a place of preparation. It is also a place of liminality and longing, the precarious bridge that links our world with the world-to-come. Our "mission" as human beings is a very challenging one. Despite the intensity of our yearning to stand in the eternal presence of God, we must strive, without pause or cessation, for self-perfection while still in the here and now. As Rabbi Tarfon states elsewhere in *Pirke Avot*, "The day is short, and the task is great" (*Avot* 2:20).

There have been, over the centuries, a large number of spiritual seekers and activists who have viewed their life's purpose as working to bring heaven and earth closer together, striving—each in his or her own small way—to narrow the metaphysical gulf between this world and the world-to-come.

For Saint Catherine of Siena (1347–80), this monumental task could be accomplished, in part, by changing our perception about the nature of the relationship between "this" world and the "next" world. She writes, "The path to heaven lies through heaven, and all the way to heaven is heaven." If we erase the (false) distinction between earth and heaven, if we view the more ennobled human actions and emotions (such as righteousness, humility, and love) as manifestations of the divine, then we will come to see that everything is holy, everything is godly.

Dorothy Day (1897–1980), a social activist and the founder of the *Catholic Worker*, took inspiration from Saint Catherine's words and devoted her life to the cause of justice and the creation of community—which she saw as the path to bridge the gap between heaven and earth. In an interview conducted toward the end of her life, Day discussed how her colleague and mentor, Peter Maurin, not only helped her with her work, but transformed the way she viewed the world:

> That's where Peter was the key; he was the one who turned my head around! I'd be out there hawking our paper, or protesting something, and then I'd want to go off and be by myself, or be with Tamar [her daughter] and no one else—but there Peter would be, reminding me of what had to be done, giving me his pep talks. I'd be grouchy, and he'd be mentioning those Bible stories and telling me, "Dorothy, this is our big chance, right now—here!" No wonder I quote Catherine of Siena at the start of *The Long Loneliness* [Day's autobiography]. I can hear Peter saying to me that there is here and there is heaven, and our job is to bring the two as close together as possible.

Day, inspired by Saint Catherine and guided by Maurin, believed that her mission in life—that the underlying, teleological purpose *of* life—was to bring the here and now into alignment with the hereafter. The duty of humanity, as well as its opportunity, is to strive to diminish the separation between "present" and "future," between "mortal" and "eternal." If heaven (or the world-to-come) represents the final, messianic realization of aspirational ideas such as justice, peace, and love, then the idea of creating a heaven on earth, or a heaven *of* earth, does not seem totally farfetched, since we can experience those realities in concrete ways during the course of our lifetimes.

Importantly, the culmination of our striving is not self-perfection—though that is essential to the messianic goal—but *social* perfection. It is the transformation of society as a whole, not just the betterment of each of us as individuals, that must be the driving force behind our most impassioned actions and our greatest aspirations.

Human beings yearn for many things: a sense of purpose, a life of meaning, the ability to be the best we can be. In the end, what we are really craving—even if it is hidden from our consciousness—is God. Unlike many other theologians of his time who tried to prove God's existence using rational arguments, Saint Augustine of Hippo (354–430) claimed that the inner hunger all of us feel is, in truth, a desire to be united with our Creator. For him, it is the universality and constancy of human yearning that is proof of God's reality. Our yearning is of an intensity and kind that no worldly possession or person could ever satisfy, and it would not have been implanted in us if it could be satiated in some other way. The only way is through God.

I have felt that hunger, and I have I seen that way.

The "mission" of life is not to create a bridge between heaven and earth; it is to experience the presence of, and develop a relationship with, the Almighty.

I know firsthand that once a relationship with God is established, it will ebb and flow in intensity, depending on who we are and where we are in our lives. It will change in character. It will nourish us if we let it, and even when we are not available to hear the call—as I myself have been, largely absent and deaf since my rabbinic burnout after years in the field—it will be waiting for us and, when we're ready, it will beckon once more.

In Psalm 63, David—who as king of Israel has all the power, riches, and lovers he could ask for—is still hungry. What he craves, however, is not more material sustenance, but God, with whom he has had a long but complicated relationship:

God, You are my God;
I search for You,
my soul thirsts for You,

my body yearns for You,
as a parched and thirsty land that has no water. (Ps. 63:2)

There is reason for hope. God desires to be united with David as well—and, if we view the flawed ruler as a metaphor for humanity, with each of *us*. Hosea, speaking for God, expresses this idea poetically:

And I will espouse you forever:
I will espouse you with righteousness and justice,
And with goodness and mercy,
And I will espouse you with faithfulness;
Then you shall be devoted to the LORD. (Hosea 2:21–22)

Why would God implant such a deep, at times disconcerting, hunger within our souls? To draw us nearer, perhaps, to bring us closer. God has given us both the appetite *and* the nourishment to satisfy our craving. Our hunger, our inner yearning to be with the Infinite One, can drive us to perfect ourselves, propel us to prepare for the encounter, even make us afraid. For fear takes us out of ourselves—to find ourselves.

What does the LORD your God demand of you? An open heart. And a brave soul.

5

A Definition of Madness

~

MY FASCINATION WITH EXTREME WEATHER predates the movie *Twister* by almost three decades. But it was that Hollywood film that brought storm chasers into the view of popular culture for the first time. How did the movie portray them? As scientists and nerds, eccentrics and thrill seekers. Who, other than an outlier or a madman, would want to aggressively pursue unpredictable forces of nature that can, within seconds, literally wipe an entire town off the face of the earth?

I had always wanted to experience a tornado firsthand, to see, hear, and feel a meteorological event that was as perilous as it was enthralling. As a child growing up in the Midwest, I'd witnessed the power of many severe thunderstorms, and I had to take shelter in our basement on numerous occasions in response to tornado warnings. I had terrifying nightmares about tornadoes pursuing me. Still, I was enthralled by them. When I was older, I grew more curious about how tornadoes formed and functioned; I wanted to try to understand the inner dynamics, not just observe the awe-inspiring external effects, of these wild and inscrutable monsters of the sky.

When I had the opportunity to write a magazine piece on a professional storm chaser from Texas, I jumped at the chance. I met Stephen Levine at his residence just outside of Dallas. The walls in his apartment were filled with photographs of dramatic lightning, interesting cloud formations, and tornadoes; bags were half-packed and ready for a road trip; on his computer screen was a page from the Storm Prediction Center (in Norman, Oklahoma) showing a map of the United States and highlighting potential regions for severe weather over the next several days. We spent the evening loading up his van with supplies we needed for the trip, which would last about a week.

I followed Stephen in a rental car and we communicated with CBS. As we drove north past the town of Moore, Oklahoma, I slowed down and gazed out the windows of my vehicle. The area looked like a war zone. A month before, a devastating F-5 tornado (the most powerful and violent level of intensity on the Fujita scale) had crossed the highway at exactly this spot and then went on to tear through the Oklahoma City suburb. Scores of people were killed and entire neighborhoods were obliterated. The damage path was still visible. A former motel was now a mass of twisted steel and shattered concrete. I felt ambivalent about what we were doing. While we were actively seeking twisters, this community had just been destroyed by one. Was I just an amoral joyrider? Was there any goal other than a thrill behind our actions?

Our initial targets were supercells, compact, high-energy thunderstorms that can develop from a towering cumulus cloud and explode sixty thousand feet or more into the atmosphere in just thirty minutes. They are the most intense of all thunderstorms, producing torrential rains, large hail, winds in excess of one hundred miles per hour, and, sometimes, tornadoes. The engine that drives these weather systems is the mesocyclone, a two- to six-mile zone of rotation within the supercell that is usually found at the southern edge of the storm. It is beneath this area (known as the "bear's cage" in chaser lingo), emerging from a structure called a wall cloud, that tornadoes can form.

We drove west across the Oklahoma panhandle and then north across the border into Liberal, Kansas, where we spent the first night. The SPC was predicting severe weather over the next few days in western Kansas and Nebraska, an area of hundreds of square miles. The next day, while we stopped at a Dairy Queen in Garden City, Kansas, Stephen pointed to an enormous, flattened sheet of cloud streaking across the sky: "That's an anvil, my friend," he said. "Let's go find us the supercell!" An anvil is made of condensed ice crystals at the tops of storms that are sprayed eastward by the jet stream, and it nearly always indicates a severe thunderstorm at its point of origin.

We drove west alongside the storm for forty or fifty miles. The temperature outside dropped precipitously. Above us, large mammatus clouds protruded from the anvil. All the signs were present for instability in the atmosphere. As we got closer to the storm's core, horizontal rain began pounding our windshields. Then came strong wind and driving hail. My heart was racing—it felt like I was heading into the belly of a gigantic beast. I could barely see Stephen's van in front of me, and soon I could no longer make out the features of the supercell's cumulonimbus tower. We punched through the shroud of precipitation and hail and, suddenly, entered sunny, clear weather. Just a mile or two from us to our south was the source of this potent energy.

We pulled off on a country road and got out of our vehicles. While its anvil unraveled across a great swath of the state of Kansas, the actual core of the supercell was only a few miles in diameter. Yet it erupted straight into the sky, a tower of churning, muscular clouds soaring sixty thousand feet. Within it was the mesocyclone. We watched the wall cloud, which had begun to rotate, and waited to see if a tornado would form below it. We could see dirt from the fields surrounding us being sucked into the storm, and we could feel the same inflow buffeting our backs, pushing us toward the core.

After ten or fifteen minutes, I saw it. At first, the funnel cloud was camouflaged by the rest of the wall cloud, but soon I could discern its discrete shape. It looked like an enormous elephant trunk, grayish and thick. A long, more narrow rope-like structure led from the funnel cloud up into the thunderhead itself, presumably stretching into the mesocyclone that was invisible from the ground. It reminded me of the handle to a vacuum cleaner. I was awestruck. I'd never witnessed anything like it before.

There was something about watching the storm that filled me with reverence. Was I in the presence of something holy?

Or was I playing with fire, pushing the boundary with something capricious, ruinous, and forbidden?

The sight before me was ominous and almost otherworldly, yet my dangerous proximity to such an overwhelming, deadly force of nature was mitigated by my adrenaline-fueled excitement. Nobody said a word. And then, within seconds, the funnel cloud dissipated into the mass of other clouds, vanishing into thin air. It never touched down, nor was its unfathomable power fully expressed. I was grateful for that. I was grateful that I never witnessed the twister churning the earth below, that I never saw it toss around trees and tractor trailers like children's toys. I was thankful that I never beheld up close something that few people ever experience and survive without deep wounds.

I was happy the tornado never touched down. At least that's what I told myself.

"What is this you have done?" (Genesis 3:13)

The second chapter in the book of Genesis presents us with a vision of human existence that is primeval and idyllic. Adam, who is created first (from the earth itself, or *adamah*), tends to the Garden of Eden in peaceful solitude. The story describes a river that flows from Eden, how it divides into four branches, and how the lands that it reaches are filled with gold, bdellium, and onyx. God tells Adam that he is free to eat from any tree in the garden he chooses, as long as it is not from the tree of the knowledge of good and evil: "For as soon as you eat of it, you shall die" (Gen. 2:17).

God does not think it is good for the man to be alone, so God brings into being other creatures to keep Adam company: "wild beasts and all the birds of the sky" (Gen. 2:19), according to the text. The man gives names to all the living creatures and lives among them. God, however, decides that creation is not yet complete and that Adam needs a different, more suitable companion. God casts a deep sleep over the man, removes one of his ribs, and forms a woman from it.

Adam and his wife (she does not yet have a name in the narrative) live, naked and without shame, in the Garden of Eden. Eventually, they encounter a mysterious serpent (*nahash*), who informs them that if they eat of the tree in the middle of the garden, they will not die, as God had warned Adam earlier. Instead, the serpent tells them, their eyes will be opened and they will be like God, knowing the difference between good and evil. The man and woman eat the fruit of the forbidden tree: "Then the eyes of both of them were opened and they perceived that they were naked; and they sewed together fig leaves and made themselves loincloths" (Gen. 3:7).

Things have changed suddenly and dramatically for the first two human beings. They now possess moral sensibility. They feel self-conscious.

Yet their lives are about to change even more dramatically.

When the man and woman hear the voice of God "moving about" in the garden, they hide among the trees. As they cower in fear and shame, God calls out to Adam and his wife, "Where are you?" (Gen. 3:9). It seems to be a leading question that has as much to do with the couple's existential state as it does with their location. Adam tells God that he was afraid because of his nakedness, and God asks Adam if he has eaten from the tree of the knowledge of good and evil. Acknowledging their transgression but avoiding an admission of guilt, Adam blames his wife, while the woman blames the serpent.

Then God asks another question, this one more multilayered than the first: "What is this you have done?" (Gen. 3:13).

A professor of mine in rabbinical school called this the most profound question ever asked in human history. What is it that Adam and Eve *have* done, and why? There is only one prohibition in the entire story of creation, and the first man and woman both break it. Is God's question an expression of incredulity and disappointment? Is it an outburst of anger? Is it a rhetorical device meant to brace them for what follows?

Whatever God's intent, the punishment for their rebellion is severe:

And to the woman He said,
"I will make most severe
Your pangs in childbearing;
In pain shall you bear children.
Yet your urge shall be for your husband,
And he shall rule over you."
To Adam He said, "Because you did as your wife said and ate of the
tree about which I commanded you, 'You shall not eat of it,'
Cursed be the ground because of you;
By toil shall you eat of it
All the days of your life:
Thorns and thistles shall it sprout for you.
But your food shall be the grasses of the field;

By the sweat of your brow
Shall you get bread to eat,
Until you return to the ground—
For from it you were taken.
For dust you are,
And to dust you shall return." (Gen. 3:16–19)

Adam and Eve have lost a paradise. The couple seem to have had it all in the Garden of Eden: serenity, innocence, and a personal relationship with God. The consequences for their sin of disobedience are greater than pain in childbirth and the need to work for food: death has become a permanent part of the human condition for the first time, and the nature of existence has changed irrevocably. To prevent them from eating of the other tree in the middle of the garden, the tree of life, and becoming immortal (and more like God), Adam and Eve are banished from Eden forever. The cost of free will and unrestrained curiosity is a life of detachment and alienation from their Creator.

Adam and Eve are punished not just for disobedience and defiance, but for striving to know things that are forbidden to them. The story asks, and raises, critical questions: Are some types of knowledge too dangerous for human beings to possess? How far are we allowed to go in our inquiries about the world and ourselves?

Whether they were driven by curiosity or seduced by the serpent, Adam and Eve have fallen from their original state of grace. What were they thinking? With so much at stake, and after being clearly and strongly forewarned by God, were they crazy?

FORBIDDEN FRUIT

The Torah tells us that Adam and Eve found the forbidden tree to be "good for eating and a delight to the eyes" (Gen. 3:6), and so they ate of its fruit. Over the centuries, commentators have speculated as to what sort of fruit it was that the archetypal couple ate. Some claim that it was a pomegranate, which is native to and common in the Middle East, seen by many as the setting for the Garden of Eden. In the Talmud, Rabbi Meir argues that the forbidden fruit was a grape, which was made into wine before its consumption, while Rabbi Nehemiah suggests that it was a fig, since the couple used fig leaves to cover their nakedness (BT Berachot 40a and Sanhedrin 70a). Perhaps the best known interpretation is that the fruit was an apple, an image that appears regularly in Western religious art. Many trace this association to the Vulgate, the Latin translation of the Bible, and linguistic similarities between the words for "evil" and "apple."

Whichever type of fruit it was, the first human beings, according to the story, clearly found it irresistible. As a metaphor, it is compelling. The one and only thing that was prohibited to them became the very thing that Adam and Eve craved most.

The meaning of "the fall" has been the subject of much discussion by thinkers and theologians. It is clear that the actions of Adam and Eve result in immeasurable loss, both to them and to their descendants. Prior to the forbidden fruit story, the man and his wife are depicted as living in a world of peace, painlessness, and "pure being," an existence that involves a direct and intimate relationship with God. According to the narrative, their only task is "to till and tend [the Garden of Eden]" (Gen. 2:15). After their act of disobedience and expulsion from the garden, Adam and Eve experience loss in physical as well as metaphysical ways: struggle, suffering, and death enter their lives, and their close, personal connection to God, now fractured, transforms irretrievably.

In light of the reality of death and the fissure in the divine-human relationship, the enormity of what has been lost is self-evident. Yet what has been *gained*?

As a consequence of Adam and Eve's behavior—and the ingestion of the fruit from the tree of the knowledge of good and evil—humans evolve from a state of ethical indifference about the world to a place of moral discrimination. In exercising freedom of choice, Adam and Eve commit a grave transgression. Yet they also become capable of making choices that are virtuous. In classical Christian theology, all human beings are viewed as inherently sinful because of the actions of Adam and Eve (an idea known as "original sin"). In contrast, Jewish thought, while conceding the human impulse toward evil (*yetzer ha-ra*), also affirms our impulse toward good (*yetzer ha-tov*). Each human being is responsible for his or her own moral character and existential destiny.

Some interpreters claim that the Genesis tale is about the discovery not of moral choice, but of sexuality. This interpretation sees the Hebrew word for "knowledge" (*da'at*) as suggestive of *carnal* knowledge, or sexual experience. The fact that our forebears try to cover their nakedness seems to support this view. Others, however, argue that it is the discovery of knowledge in general, not in a specific form (moral or sexual), that is the nexus of the narrative. In the Bible, the phrase "good and evil" (*tov v'ra*) can mean "everything." With this understanding, Adam and Eve eat of the tree of "omniscience" and, having tasted its mind-expanding fruit, will from that moment forward strive to know everything—that is, become like God. In this sense, hubris and self-deification, not disobedience and defiance, are at the heart of their sin.

Whether it is moral, sexual, or general knowledge that is contained in, and represented by, the forbidden fruit, its consumption leads to mortality and alienation. Yet humanity's defiance of the divine command also results in liberation and growth. By acting with free will, Adam and Eve begin the process of individuation from God, psychologically and existentially. They are now on their own. The story offers us a portrait of God that is contradictory in nature. While God seems to provide Adam and Eve with the possibility of remaining in Eden, God also (intentionally?) tempts them with the tree of knowledge. When they succumb to its fruit, they are punished.

The biblical image of human nature is contradictory as well. The philosopher Martin Buber (1878–1965) tries to convey the essence of this duality:

> At the end of the first creation story [Gen. 1:1–2:4] stands a double blessing—of the first man and the first Shabbat; at the end of the second creation story [Gen. 2:5–3:24] stands a double curse—on the first man and the earth. Between both stands Sin. Natural man is established by a blessing; historical man by a curse. Both together form the dual nature and the dual fate of man. (*Werke*, vol. 2)

Commentators and thinkers have long observed that there are two very different creation stories in the book of Genesis, and most modern Bible scholars argue that they were written by two separate authors (or sets of authors). As evidence for this latter view, scholars highlight several important distinctions: style and language; descriptions of the beginning of heaven and earth; the names and actions of God; the nature of Adam (and the lack of an Eve in the first creation story); and how the narratives end.

The authorship of the Genesis stories notwithstanding, the fact is that those who ultimately compiled the Hebrew canon chose to include both of them together. For Buber, it is only when we read the creation stories as a totality—a single, interrelated narrative—that we can fully understand their meaning and import. The first story depicts humanity (represented by Adam) as meritorious and worthy of blessing; the second story portrays humanity as sinful and condemnable. The Torah, as Buber interprets it, conveys a message about and to human beings: our nature is divided, as is our fate.

In an *aggadah* (talmudic homily) that predates Buber by many centuries, we find a scene about Adam and Eve that captures the beauty as well as the danger of human duality. It takes place in the aftermath of the forbidden fruit episode and the couple's expulsion from Eden. It is a vision of their first experience of night:

> Our masters taught: When Adam saw the sun sinking in the sky before him and the day gradually diminishing, he said, "Woe is me! Perhaps because I acted offensively, the world around me is growing darker and darker, and it is about to return to chaos and confusion— indeed, this is the death that Heaven has decreed for me." So he sat down to fast and to weep throughout the night, while Eve wept beside him. But when the dawn began slowly rising like a column, he said, "Such is the way of nature, and I did not realize it." Then he proceeded to offer up a bullock. (BT Avodah Zarah 8a)

Adam witnesses his first dusk with a sense of dread and foreboding. As the sun sets over the world and the light of day gives way to the darkness of night, he fears not only that existence is returning to its primordial state of anarchy and emptiness, but that he is the direct cause of its dissolution. Adam foresees, in the twilight, the realization of death that

God had decreed after he ate from the tree of knowledge. In an act of petition and, it appears, an expression of contrition, Adam—now joined by Eve—fasts and weeps throughout the night. It is a fervent and fevered attempt to stave off doom.

When dawn arrives, light returns, and the world does not collapse into entropy, Adam has an epiphany. He comes to realize that the cycle of light and darkness, life and death, is the natural order of things. While the sunset does not usher in Adam's demise, he will still die at some point in the future. And while daybreak rises "like a column," it will fall soon enough, and it will be followed by yet another night. Adam accepts this cycle of nature, and he offers a sacrifice—the earliest form of religious expression—to convey his relief, gratitude, and reverence in the face of this newfound truth. But to whom is Adam directing his sacrifice—to the Creator, or to creation *itself*?

The answer is not clear in the story. Just as Adam mistakes night and darkness for punishment and death, perhaps he misinterprets monotheism for pantheism. Rather than seeing nature's cycles as the result of divine design (and extolling God for their power and beauty), he may see nature itself as divine and worthy of praise and reverence. (In another version of the *aggadah*, Adam observes a holiday at the end of the winter solstice, the darkest time of the year.) The fact that the sages included this story in the tractate "Idolatry" suggests how they likely interpreted Adam's actions.

The duality in the creation stories referred to by Buber is present in this tale as well. Immediately after their banishment from Eden, Adam and Eve continue to err and to commit grave sins. Yet they also evolve and mature. This story shows how the couple grow in their perception of the world, how they gain a new perspective on reality. It also highlights the cyclical, and paradoxical, nature of humanity itself, how our mistakes can be accompanied by insights, our knowledge by overreach and transgression.

The Torah contains other, lesser known but compelling stories about forbidden knowledge. Toward the end of the book of Exodus, just after Moses shatters the divine tablets during the golden calf episode, he asks God for assurance that God will lead the people of Israel as they continue their journey to the Promised Land. Moses is anxious in the wake of the Israelites' challenge to his own leadership, and God agrees to his request: "And the LORD said to Moses, 'I will also do this thing that you have asked; for you have truly gained My favor and I have singled you out by name'" (Exod. 33:17).

Emboldened by God's positive words about his leadership, Moses—who has devoted life and limb to serving God as an intermediary—pleads for something he has never before demanded: "Oh, let me behold Your glory!" (Exod. 33:18).

What Moses asks for, specifically, is a firsthand experience of God's *kavod*. While the Hebrew word is often translated as "glory," its precise meaning is unclear. The root letters of *kavod* are connected to weightiness or gravity, but the word seems to relate to God's nature, essence, or interior identity. Moses, like Adam and Eve, strives for direct knowledge of something that, as God warns him, is forbidden to him:

And He answered, "I will make all My goodness pass before you, and I will proclaim before you the name LORD, and the grace that I grant and the compassion that I show. But," He said, "you cannot see My face, for man may not see Me and live." And the LORD said, "See, there is a place near Me. Station yourself on the rock and, as My glory [*kavod*] passes by, I will put you in a cleft of the rock and shield you with My hand until I have passed by. Then I will take My hand away and you will see My back; but My face must not be seen." (Exod. 33:19–23)

Up to this point in the Exodus narrative, Moses has known God through many and varied guises: creator, protector, redeemer, lawgiver, ruler. Yet whenever the divine presence seems to erupt into history most profoundly and dramatically, it is concealed by fire, smoke, clouds, and unpronounceable names. Moses wants more. He wants *clarity*. Moses asks God to disclose God's true nature and identity; the ineffable name and transcendent reality that were revealed to him through the burning bush (discussed in chapter 2) have left him unfulfilled, inquisitive, and restless.

Moses does not get what he asks for, though he does get a taste of the *kavod* he craves to encounter. Rather than being allowed to behold God's glory or "face," he is permitted only to see God's "back." God keeps Moses at a careful distance from the divine presence, ordering him to stand on a rock near God; when the *kavod* passes by, God will put Moses in a cleft of the rock and shield him with God's hand. Then God will remove the divine hand and Moses will get a glimpse of God's back.

This is far from the clarity about God's nature that Moses desires. The prophet's mountaintop encounter with God is an indirect one, and his knowledge about God's essence remains limited. In the end, the Torah offers little more than anthropomorphic imagery and metaphor about the divine identity. (According to Rashi, Moses sees the knot of God's tefillin as God's *kavod* passes by.) The finite human mind will never be able to fathom the mystery of the Infinite One. God is forever beyond us.

Despite all of the barriers and limitations, Moses does receive a degree of understanding. As he descends Mount Sinai with two new tablets, the text tells us that the skin on Moses's face is "radiant" (Exod. 34:29). The radiance that emanates from Moses, described by commentators and depicted by artists such as Michelangelo and Rembrandt, suggests that Moses now possesses a kind of "enlightenment" that separates the prophet from those around him. Yet the scene also implies that there is a very fine line—as we saw in the tale of Adam and Eve—between the reward of illumination and the risk of annihilation. Forbidden knowledge is as dangerous as it is seductive.

The Talmud states that while it is permissible to inquire about the events of the first six days of creation, it is forbidden to inquire into *ma'aseh bereshit*, that which occurred prior to the creation of the world (BT Hagigah 11b). For the sages, esoteric speculation about the origins of creation borders on self-deification, that is, placing oneself in the position of God. The rabbinic authorities often used the term *ma'aseh bereshit* as a euphemism for mysticism in general; the pursuit of mystical knowledge was seen, in their eyes, as an alarmingly subversive endeavor and a transgressive distraction from normative modes of religious observance. The talmudic injunction, then, is directed not just against a specific idea, but against an entire category of cognitive exploration.

The biblical and later religious traditions clearly urge us to exercise caution when, or *before*, we strive for certain types of knowledge. While the rewards can be transformative (insight, perspective, maturity), the risks are profound and dangerous (transgression, idolatry, and death). The same impulse that can lead to freedom and growth can also corrupt our minds, pollute our souls, and mutate our world.

LIBERATION AND LIMITS

The tension between our seemingly insatiable curiosity and hunger for knowledge and the sometimes deleterious consequences of our heedless acquisition of that objective is not limited to the world of religion. In his 1996 book *Forbidden Knowledge,* the literary scholar and social critic Roger Shattuck (1923–2005) raises vital questions about the apparent disconnect between knowledge and morality:

> Are there things we should not know? Can anyone or any institution, in this culture of unfettered enterprise and growth, seriously propose limits on knowledge? Have we lost the capacity to perceive and honor the moral dimensions of such questions? Our increasingly bold discoveries of the secrets of nature may have reached the point where that knowledge is bringing us more problems than solutions. . . . Not only the most barbarous nations but also the most civilized expend vast resources to develop nuclear and biological weapons of unthinkable destructive force. Genetic research raises the remote prospect of choosing our children's physical and mental endowment like wallpaper patterns. The invasive presence of audio-visual media in our lives from earliest infancy threatens to shape our character and behavior as forcefully as genetic manipulation. In our quest for energy sources, we may be reducing the life span of our planet. . . . Our greatest blessings confound us.

A great deal of good has resulted from our understanding—and our reconfiguring—of the world around us. Our insights and advancements have freed us in many ways from the constraints that our forebears had to face.

Yet how do we reconcile liberation with limits?

Since Shattuck wrote those words, our technological and scientific knowledge has grown qualitatively and quantitatively—and our world has become more frightening. Rogue states try to acquire nuclear weapons and terrorists scheme to make dirty bombs. Genetic engineering has made modified food, cloning, and other forms of manipulation almost commonplace. The Internet, smart phones, and other digital devices have made personal information and private images publicly accessible through search engines and social media. Climate change, and its disastrous, long-term effects on the earth, is a reality that is getting worse.

Some argue that we have become too smart too quickly, that while humanity has progressed intellectually beyond our wildest dreams, our *moral* knowledge has not evolved in a similar way. As we have strived to understand and improve our world—as we have, in effect, created a "new" world—we have not been nearly as passionate, or as diligent, about weighing the external as well as the internal consequences of our insights and achievements. And those consequences are not always positive ones.

Western culture, and the thinkers, writers, and artists who helped to shape it, has grappled with the themes of liberation, limits, and dangerous knowledge for many centuries. The actions of two important figures from classical Greek mythology, Prometheus and Pandora, highlight these ideas in vivid ways. Prometheus is a Titan and a friend of early humanity. After Prometheus angers Zeus with an act of trickery, Zeus creates pain and sorrow for humanity, and he hides fire from them. Yet Prometheus steals it back and returns the secret of fire to our ancestors. Now even more enraged, Zeus sentences Prometheus to eternal torment for his defiance and transgression. The immortal Titan is bound to a rock, where an eagle feeds on his liver forever.

There have been many interpretations of what the fire represents: creativity, technical skill, science, language, consciousness. By fearlessly wresting away the knowledge that Zeus conceals and withholds from humanity, Prometheus becomes our heroic liberator, freeing us from ignorance, dependence, and subservience.

But the story does not end on the rock.

In further retaliation for Prometheus's defiance, Zeus sends Pandora (the first woman) to tempt the Titan's brother, Epimetheus. Pandora brings a jar with her that was given to her by the gods and that contains, she thinks, a collection of many and varied "gifts." When Epimetheus falls prey to her charms, Pandora—curious about the contents of the vessel that she was instructed to give to him—removes the lid of the jar and releases all manner of evil, suffering, and disease into the world.

The grave effects of Pandora's action seem to neutralize, or eliminate, any benefits that Prometheus bestows through his gift of fire earlier in the myth.

The relationship of the two stories underscores the challenges of liberation and limits. It is noteworthy that in later, more "sanitized" versions of the Prometheus story, there is no mention of the interrelated tale involving Pandora; the focus is squarely on Prometheus's heroic raid on Mount Olympus and the liberating fire he secures for humanity. Yet if we separate the positive aspects of fire from the negative consequences of its acquisition, we distort the myth irreparably. The two stories form a single narrative that is not just about humanity's triumph over ignorance and darkness; it is also meant as a warning, a cautionary tale about the dangers of overreach and presumption.

There are a number of similarities between the Greek myth of Prometheus and Pandora and the Genesis story of Adam and Eve: forbidden knowledge, curiosity, transgression, free will, the origin of evil and suffering, and unintended consequences. At their core, the myths express a complex of ideas linked to the notion of *taboo*.

Cultural anthropologists have observed that a taboo usually relates to an object, place, individual, or action in which there is no differentiation between the sacred and the forbidden. The allure of holiness, fused with the threat of contamination, necessitates the existence of a protective force, something that insulates the sacred in the person or object from violation or pollution. Yet the force of taboo also protects *us* from its forbidding but almost irresistible power. Sigmund Freud (1856–1939) was extremely interested in the concept of taboo, and in *Totem and Taboo* he writes about it in the context of human psychology: "Taboos are very ancient prohibitions which at one time were forced upon a generation of primitive people from without, that is, they probably were forcibly impressed upon them by an earlier generation. These prohibitions concerned actions for which there existed a strong desire."

Whether it is the secret of fire or fruit from the tree of the knowledge of good and evil, both the Greek and the biblical stories wrestle with the dilemma of human curiosity about something that is simultaneously seductive and dangerous—in short, something that is taboo. In *The Canterbury Tales*, Geoffrey Chaucer (1343–1400) captures the psychology of curiosity and the futility of attempts to control human craving: "Forbede us thyng, / and that desiren we" ("The Wife of Bath's Tale").

In the Genesis story, God forbids Adam and Eve only one thing in the paradise that they live in—the fruit of the tree of knowledge. After they (predictably) eat it, God asks them incredulously, "What is this you have done?" (Gen. 3:13).

In light of the stories, ideas, and observations about forbidden knowledge in this chapter, which is "crazier"—the actions of Adam and Eve, or God's question?

While a vast corpus of commentaries had been written on the Adam and Eve myth by the time of John Milton (1608–74), it wasn't until the poet wrote *Paradise Lost* that a new literary version of the tale was created. Milton opens his epic poem not with the creation story, but with Satan, by then the standard Christian analogue for the enigmatic *nahash* referred to in the third chapter of Genesis. Satan has been cast out of heaven as punishment for an attempted revolt against God. He and his followers gather in hell and plot revenge on a new world (Eden) that God has created after their uprising. As Satan ventures forth to find the location of the paradisiacal new world, God looks down from heaven, observes Satan nearing the garden, and foresees that Adam and Eve will succumb to temptation and fall, ushering into the world sin and death:

> Of Man's first disobedience, and the fruit
> Of that forbidden tree, whose mortal taste
> Brought death into the world, and all our woe,

With loss of Eden ...
Sing, Heav'nly Muse, ... (1.1–4, 6)

In relation to the idea of forbidden knowledge that is so central to these verses, ought we to place emphasis on the action that is *forbidden*, or on the *knowledge* that the fruit represents? In other words, is it an act of disobedience and transgression or the acquisition of dangerous knowledge that results in the loss of paradise for Adam, Eve, and all the rest of us to come? Milton leaves the answer ambiguous here. Elsewhere in the poem, however, he makes it clear that rebellion alone is not our only sin.

Milton devotes four books of *Paradise Lost* to exchanges between Adam and Eve and the archangel Raphael, who has been sent by God on a mission to warn Adam, in particular, to "beware / He swerve not" (5.237–38). Yet before Raphael can fulfill his charge, Adam starts asking questions about the nature of heaven and how worldly life compares to "things above this World" (5.455). Adam expresses more than mere curiosity about what life is like in heaven; he conveys a restlessness and dissatisfaction about his lot even as he and Eve live without a care in the heart of paradise.

After Raphael recounts the story of creation to the couple, replete with images both awe-inspiring and almost fantastical, Adam still yearns to know more about the mysteries of the universe and the nature of divinity. The archangel has had enough. He warns Adam not to strive to know things that are beyond his reach, and he urges Adam to be humble about his intellectual capacities and content with his life on the earth:

Heav'n is for thee too high
To know what passes there; be lowly wise:
Think only what concerns thee and thy being;
Dream not of other worlds, what creatures there
Live, in what state, condition, or degree,
Contented that thus far hath been reveal'd
Not of Earth only but of highest Heav'n. (8.172–78)

Milton, using the voice of Raphael, seems to offer a message about hubris and human striving. Like Adam (or Moses, who, as we have seen, yearned to experience God's *kavod* face-to-face), all human beings are discontent with our lot—we want more than what we have, we crave that which is not ours, we covet those things that are different and other. When they are forbidden to us, we desire them even more. Our hunger for the fascinating usually triumphs over our respect for the fearful.

One hundred and fifty years after the publication of *Paradise Lost*, another English author, Mary Shelley (1797–1851), wrote a Gothic novel about forbidden knowledge that has had wide-ranging influence not only on Western literature but on the popular imagination: *Frankenstein; or, The Modern Prometheus*. On the title page of the first edition of Shelley's novel, she includes an epigraph from *Paradise Lost*:

> Did I request thee, Maker, from my clay
> To mould me Man, did I solicit thee
> From darkness to promote me—? (10.743–45)

These are the words that Adam uses to challenge his Creator. While "the creature" in *Frankenstein* does not have a name, it essentially asks the same question of its own creator, Dr. Victor Frankenstein. Both Adam and the creature are unhappy with their lives. They crave *more*. And both wonder why they were brought into a world of yearning and pain without their consent—and then abandoned, as they perceive their situations, and left to fend for themselves. *Paradise Lost* and *Frankenstein* are literary works, but they are also commentaries on the tree of knowledge myth in Genesis, and they highlight the tensions between creation and creator, liberation and limits.

The protagonist of Shelley's novel, Victor Frankenstein, is a young and unknown scientist, but a man with colossal ambition. He seeks to understand the mystery of creation, and with zeal and resolve (and, ultimately, recklessness) he creates life, a monster made from cadavers and animated by electricity. But Frankenstein's artificial generation of life brings with it grave consequences. The monster commits four horrific murders of those whom Frankenstein loves most. By violating the laws of nature—

and playing the role of God—Frankenstein has brought about death, not life. He is as responsible as the creature for the outcome. Creation and creator are damned.

Near the end of his life in the wastes of the High Arctic, and in relentless, monomaniacal pursuit of the monster that he has brought into being, Frankenstein uses his own life as a tragic example of how heedless ambition and thoughtless curiosity will lead only to mayhem, misery, and even madness: "Learn from me how dangerous is the acquirement of knowledge, and how much happier that man is who believes his native town to be the world, than he who aspires to become greater than his nature will allow."

Frankenstein is a warning about the dangers of ambition and overreach, about what can happen when human beings thrust aside humility and limits in a hell-bent search for knowledge and experience. We may want the reward without the responsibility, but our hubris and excess can have unintended, and at times dire, consequences. Whether it is Adam in the Garden of Eden or the person who lives contentedly in his "native town," we'd be mad to give up peaceful satisfaction for ceaseless, boundless striving.

In Jewish folklore, the golem is a mythical being made of clay that is conjured into life by means of esoteric rituals, mysterious incantations, and the invocation of secret names. Like the monster in *Frankenstein*, the golem is a creature that is enormously powerful, but it is also uncontrollable and potentially destructive. As a metaphor, the golem is apt to the themes in this chapter. While the pursuit and acquisition of knowledge, even knowledge that is dangerous, can sometimes lift our souls and aid our world, it can also—despite our best intentions—damage or destroy them.

There is something very alluring about powerful and uncontrollable things, and despite our best intentions, it is often hard to resist our desire to experience, encounter, or create them. I know that that impulse is very much at work in my fascination with severe weather and storm chasing. My craving to bear witness to the might and majesty of tornadoes usually overrides any concerns I might have about the moral nature of the activity itself. Does storm chasing serve any real purpose beyond satisfying my own curiosity and providing me with a jolt of adrenaline? Does it help anyone?

In the foreword to *Forbidden Knowledge*, Shattuck describes his experience of flying over Hiroshima as a young combat pilot a few weeks after the atomic bomb was dropped there. That vision of total destruction haunted him for decades. Despite the fact that the two atomic bombs that were dropped on Japan likely ended the Second World War, Shattuck writes that the acquisition and development of nuclear energy also *changed* the world, and not necessarily for the better:

> Marked by that series of events, I have lived out my biblical portion of years with a warning light constantly flashing in my peripheral vision. It continues to signal that we have strayed off course, that some mechanism has malfunctioned.... The warning light still flashes. I have come to believe that its signal refers not only to the destructive forces we have conjured out of the atom but even more essentially to a condition we have lived with always: the perils and temptations of forbidden knowledge.

Whatever good the modern-day golem of nuclear power has brought about might very well be outweighed by the almost unfathomable, and potentially uncontrollable, annihilative force that it can unleash. Yet our desire to touch that which is perilous, to grasp that which is forbidden, always seems to mitigate this latter concern. In the end, we take our chances whenever we embark on the pursuit of knowledge, since we can never be fully certain where our discoveries will take us. Whether our actions result in a revelation of light or a disclosure of darkness is not ultimately in our hands.

6

Separation Anxiety

I HAVE USUALLY SOUGHT GOD through extreme experiences, on mountain peaks, and in exotic lands. As a Jew, and as a congregational rabbi for much of my professional life, that can pose problems. Judaism is a religious tradition in which peoplehood is a powerful feature and a primary focus. Consequently, there is a basic disconnect between serving as the spiritual leader of a Jewish community and being pulled so forcefully toward solitary adventures. I have struggled for two decades to make peace between the call of the wild and the call of my faith. And because I have often looked for a sense of spiritual connection, not in human relationships, but through encounters with the sublime, I have very frequently felt, and continue to feel, like an outlier among my own people.

My path has been a lonely one, but it has felt authentic to me. Perhaps I have not felt comfortable enough to expose myself to others. Maybe I have been afraid of letting go of control. Or maybe my childhood heart operation made me feel different and led me to create unconscious barriers with others. Whatever the reason, it has always been easier for me to seek adventures without rather than within.

While I have tried to be authentic to myself, one experience showed me the limits of my solitary journey—and the rewards of a journey with another person.

Several years into my tenure as the senior rabbi of my congregation, I traveled one summer to the Faroe Islands. The Faroes are an archipelago of islands in the North Atlantic, roughly midway between Norway and Iceland. Today they are a territory of Denmark, but the Faroe Islands were first settled by Irish monks, followed by the Vikings. They are a place of stark, raw beauty, and they are sparsely populated. I hiked over hills so verdant and misty they seemed otherworldly, and along sheer cliffs dotted with puffins and surrounded by grey seals and pilot whales. There was a quiet but intense spirituality that suffused the land and the sea. It was a spirituality of solitude.

I felt a kinship with that sense of solitariness. It didn't exactly make me feel uplifted, but it did seem to speak to a part of my soul that only nature could.

When I returned to New York City at the end of the summer (with no small measure of reluctance), one of my first tasks as a congregational rabbi was to welcome new members who had joined our synagogue. One of them, Tori, was a literary agent and a self-proclaimed atheist and provocateur. We instantly took a liking to each other. If we weren't discussing the ever-changing state of the publishing industry, we were talking about—or, more accurately, arguing over—the existence of God. Tori's challenges to theism were thoughtful and sound, and I offered a defense of my belief, and a critique of atheism, that she found equally compelling. Our views on God couldn't have been more different and divergent, but our theological exchanges (at the synagogue, at restaurants, and over dry martinis) were always revivifying, enlightening, and fun.

I respected Tori and I knew that she respected me. Tori was smart, and it was obvious that she had thought about spiritual matters for a very long time. Perhaps for that reason, I kept debating her because I wanted to "win," to bring over this new congregant to the side of truth. Although we saw validity in one another's arguments, it became increasingly clear as time went on that neither of us was going to budge from our fundamental positions. And it raised a larger issue for me: What is, or ought to be, my job as a rabbi within the context of a spiritual community? Should my conversations, teachings, and sermons be devoted to promoting the Jewish belief in God?

I eventually came to see the folly of my mission, how I'd misunderstood and misperceived the true nature of my work as a spiritual leader. I had been so busy debating and arguing with Tori about God's existence that I'd hidden from myself the fact that our engagement *itself* was spiritual. The distance between the two of us was not vast, and our separation was mostly illusory. I respected, even loved Tori, and I saw the divine image that was within her—even if she herself adamantly denied its existence.

Tori and I had formed a sacred connection, an I-thou relationship. It wasn't the spirituality of solitude that I'd experienced in the Faroe Islands—it was a spirituality of a completely different order. Despite the apparent, surface divide between us, we were bound by a faith tradition anchored in dialogue rather than dogma; by an iconoclastic impulse to overturn decorum in pursuit of knowledge and wisdom; by an embrace of pluralism and a commitment to community, even if some of our particular views (and our respective levels of commitment) differed in significant ways.

It was strange for me to feel that my soul was being nourished, not by nature, but by another human being. It was new and refreshing. And it was less lonely.

Since my experience with Tori, I have tried to understand "Torah" in its broadest sense, as an impassioned and *communal* search for meaning and purpose. I have attempted to become more tolerant and open, not only to divergent opinions, but also to the very presence of other people on my spiritual path—to see them not as threats to my privacy, but as assets to my inner development. When I succeed—and it is not easy—I am often reminded of a verse from *Pirke Avot*, a teaching that says far more about relationships than about mountaintops or oceans: "When two sit together and exchange words of Torah, then the divine presence dwells with them" (*Avot* 3:3).

It is a spirituality of community, not of isolation, that is my new goal.

"My God, my God, why have You abandoned me?" (Psalms 22:2)

The book of Psalms contains 150 discrete yet interrelated expressions of the emotional and existential vicissitudes of the human journey. Whether it is fear and angst, remorse and contrition, loneliness and lamentation, or gratitude and ecstatic joy, it seems as if there is a psalm for almost any experience or feeling imaginable. The book of Psalms is traditionally ascribed to David, Israel's ancient king. While modern biblical scholars dispute David's authorship, his colorful personality, intense passions, and complex life certainly seem to fit with many of the book's themes and concerns.

A large number of questions are voiced throughout the book. To me, perhaps the most compelling and resonant of all of them is the question that begins Psalm 22: "My God, my God, why have You abandoned me?" (Ps. 22:2) We do not know what exactly the context was for the author of these words, or what motivated a question of such pathos and pain. The tone of the psalm is, initially, anguished and forlorn. Does the author feel alone? Afraid? Forsaken? *Abused?*

When Jesus is dying on the cross, he asks the same question using Aramaic and Hebrew words, the vernacular of his time. In the Christian tradition, Jesus is resurrected three days later and speaks again, but no longer as a human being. For those who do not believe in the divinity of Jesus (or in his resurrection), his seven last words on the cross are noteworthy nonetheless. Why does Jesus pose a question, rather than make an affirmation, with his final breath? What is the significance of the fact that Jesus utters a verse from Hebrew Scripture instead of saying something original and personal? Is Jesus's last experience of mortal life that of doubt and despair rather than faith?

Psalm 22, in my view, is suggestive of a profound theological idea in Judaism: *hester panim*, or the "hiding" of God's face. This concept traces back to a scene at the end of the book of Deuteronomy. Moses is in his final days. In addition to preparing for his death, appointing Joshua as his successor, and giving instructions to the new leader and the Levites, Moses listens to God's description of the future of his people. It is a troubling prophecy about idolatry, ingratitude, and mutual abandonment:

> The LORD said to Moses: You are soon to lie with your fathers. This people will thereupon go astray after the alien gods in their midst, in the land that they are about to enter; they will forsake Me and break My covenant that I made with them. Then My anger will flare up against them, and I will abandon them and hide My countenance from them. They shall be ready prey; and many evils and troubles shall befall them. And they shall say on that day, "Surely it is because our God is not in our midst that these evils have befallen us." (Deut. 31:16–17)

The expression *hide MY countenance* is found nowhere else in the Torah, but it does appear in several other places in the Hebrew Bible (Isa. 8:17, Mic. 3:4, Ps. 13:2, and elsewhere). Just as Israel's experience of slavery in Egypt becomes a metaphor for bondage and oppression more generally in later Jewish thought and liturgy, so does this vision of God's detachment and separation from Israel become a reference point, and a recurring motif, in later biblical literature. But what exactly does it mean?

MUTUALLY ASSURED ESTRANGEMENT

Most modern Bible scholars think that the book of Deuteronomy was written by a group or movement of authors with a particular theological perspective, one that is known as the "Deuteronomic worldview." The last book of the Torah is different not only in tone and focus from the first four; it is also different in its unique, and uniform, point of view. While in the book of Genesis we read about Abraham's submission to God in one chapter (e.g., his near sacrifice of his son Isaac) and his independence, even defiance of God in another (e.g., his arguing with God during the Sodom and Gomorrah episode), in Deuteronomy the message of the book is consistent, clear, and unyielding: Israel's misfortunes, no matter how great, are the direct result of its own sins.

There are several ways of interpreting the concept of *hester panim* that is first referenced in chapter 31 of Deuteronomy. The first interpretation is the Deuteronomic view itself, namely, that God has hidden the divine countenance from Israel because its people have pursued foreign gods and broken the covenant. Under the terms of the covenant, God has promised them the land of Canaan and a special bond with the divine, but the promise is conditional: if the People of Israel are not faithful to God and the commandments that bind them to God, they will lose the land and experience hardship. When the Israelites forsake God in the verses above, God turns the divine countenance away from them.

In the biblical context, *hester panim* relates to divine punishment. The "evils and troubles" that befall the Israelites occur because God has withdrawn from them—and has removed, out of anger, the divine protection that had previously kept them safe from injury and harm. God may not be the active and overt cause of Israel's suffering, but God's *inaction* is forceful, deliberate, and punitive.

There are still people who believe in this ancient idea of passive punishment. I have personally encountered Jews from Skokie to Samarkand who have tried to explain the horrors of the Holocaust, for example, using Deuteronomic principles: God withheld protection from European Jews because many of them were assimilationist; because they were nonobservant; because the parchment inside their mezuzahs wasn't kosher. God did not "cause" the Holocaust but, by not intervening, God allowed it to occur.

The Jews were victims, not of the Nazis, but of divine detachment.

Serious religious thinkers, especially post-Holocaust theologians, have great difficulty believing in a God who would choose *not* to save innocent men, women, and children from the gas chambers and who would instead—as an act of retribution—turn away and hide the divine countenance. Some of these thinkers argue that, after Auschwitz, we are left with only two ways of conceiving of the Deity: God is either limited or abusive. With regard to the first alternative, how can God be all three "omnis"—omnibenevolent, omniscient, and omnipotent—at the same time? If God is all-good and all-seeing, it would be absurd to think that God would *willingly* permit evil and injustice in the world. Yet evil and injustice do exist, and at times even thrive, which makes God either amoral or blind. God cannot be as powerful as our forebears once imagined. Or as aware. Or as good. One of them has to go.

In his book *Facing the Abusing God*, David Blumenthal argues that we should reject not the idea of God's power, but that of God's goodness. In a post-Holocaust world, writes Blumenthal, we can have faith only if we admit that while God is often loving and kind, God is also capable of perpetrating (and allowing) acts that are so evil and unjust they can only be described as *abusive*. Throughout history, God has worked "wondrously through us" but also "awfully against us." God is not all-good, but God is real, and we must accept God for who God is if we want to have a relationship with the divine. To engage with God, according to Blumenthal, does not mean that we agree with God's actions. In fact, Blumenthal advocates a "theology of protest."

Like others, I am not satisfied (intellectually or emotionally) with a God who is capricious, limited, or abusive. There is a second way to interpret the concept of *hester panim* that is more compelling, one that makes us, not God, fundamentally responsible for the loneliness and pain that we often experience in our lives. When bad things happen to us, they are not an expression of divine punishment. Instead, they are a consequence of our own misdeeds. While this view embraces the covenantal relationship between God and humanity, it claims that *we* are the ones who distance ourselves from God, not the other way around (as is the case in the first interpretation). When we transgress, when we are unfaithful to the covenant, that bond, as in a marriage, will be broken.

Yet God does not turn away from us—we turn away from God. The detachment and separation we feel are our responsibility, and ours alone. God does not "hide" from us: we shut God out or let God in depending on our own behavior. Human freedom is the dynamic force that grounds and guides the covenantal relationship; in order to preserve and honor our free will, God does not intervene in our lives or intrude into history. With this interpretation, *hester panim* relates far more to us than it does to God.

A third way of interpreting *hester panim* is linked with perception, or misperception. The omnibenevolent, omniscient, and omnipotent God of religious tradition is also usually thought of as omni*present*—God never "hides" at all. What does get clouded, or at times blinded, is only our *perception* of God's presence. We may not be able to see God through the shadows and fog of the human condition, but that does not mean that God is not there. In chapter 28 of the book of Genesis, Jacob is in a dark place. He is on the run from his brother Esau's wrath, after having stolen both his birthright and their father's blessing. Jacob is afraid and alone. God has been absent from the narrative for almost three chapters and, Jacob surely perceives, from his life as well.

On his journey from Beersheba (site of his immoral past) to Haran (site of his uncertain future), Jacob comes upon "a certain place" and stops for the night. Filled with anxiety and a sense of desolation, Jacob places a stone under his head as a pillow, falls asleep, and has a dream. He sees a stairway or a ladder that reaches from the earth to the sky, and "angels of God were going up and down on it" (Gen. 28:12). In the dream, God stands next to Jacob, and God assures him that he will not be abandoned:

I am the LORD, the God of your father Abraham and the God of Isaac: the ground on which you are lying I will assign to you and to your offspring. . . . Remember, I am with you: I will protect you wherever you go and will bring you back to this land. I will not leave you until I have done what I have promised you. (Gen. 28:13–15)

While Jacob does not verbalize his fears or his sense of being forsaken by God, these words certainly suggest that God is well aware of the future patriarch's psycho-spiritual condition. God's promise links the destiny of Jacob to that of his father and grandfather, offers Jacob reassurance that God is and will be with him, and affirms a future of divine protection. After this theophany, Jacob has an epiphany:

Jacob awoke from his sleep and said, "Surely the LORD is present in this place, and I did not know it!" Shaken, he said, "How awesome is this place! This is none other than the abode of God, and that is the gateway to heaven." Early in the morning, Jacob took the stone that he had put under his head and set it up as a pillar and poured oil on the top of it. He named that site Bethel. (Gen. 28:16–19)

Jacob's dream, ironically, "wakes" him to God's presence in his life. The shaken Jacob concedes his blindness and gains a fresh perception of reality—his eyes are now open. The object that seemed more like a gravestone than a pillow suddenly transforms into an altar; Jacob's metaphorical death leads to spiritual rebirth. When Jacob acknowledges that God was never truly "hidden," when the illusion of God's absence is shattered with the dawn, Jacob is ready to continue on his journey. Shortly after this scene, several positive, even epic events occur in Jacob's life: he wrestles to a stalemate with a powerful and mysterious being, receives a sacred blessing, becomes Israel, reconciles with Esau, and moves forward as the next patriarch of his people.

The experience of *hester panim* is connected to who we are and the way we view the world. While our sense of God's absence is the result of our own inaccurate or errant perception, that perception can be changed. Rabbi Menachem Mendel of Kotsk (1787–1859), an important and provocative Hasidic mystic, asks the question "Where is God?" He then provides an answer: "In the place where he is given entry." The Kotsker Rebbe also offers the following teaching: "One who does not see the Omnipresent in every place will not see him in any place." Whether or not God is present in our lives is up to us. The paradox of a transcendent deity is that even as God is hidden from the world, God is present everywhere in it. If we cannot feel God, it is because we are not open enough for God to enter our souls. If we cannot see God, it is not because we are looking in the wrong places, but because we are not looking with correct vision.

There is a fourth interpretation of *hester panim*, one that affirms God's hiddenness but that does not attribute it to divine punishment, human sin, or misperception. Rather than focusing on the absence of the divine presence, this mystical approach focuses on the presence of the divine *absence*. In this way, *hester panim* does not have to be a negative experience—it can be a spiritual one. In chapter 2 I discussed the concept of *ayin*, or holy "nothingness," in the thought of the Great Maggid. For him, *ayin* is both a spiritual state and a path to God, a mystical phenomenon that empties a person's mind and, simultaneously, transforms that individual into a vessel for the divine. While the end result of *ayin* is communion with God, *ayin* begins with an experience of radical distance and division, an encounter where God is anything but present.

There are strong echoes of these ideas in the writings of Saint John of the Cross (1542–91). In his famous poem "The Dark Night of the Soul," Saint John uses the motif of "night" not just as a background image, but as the means by which a human being may encounter God. The spiritual path, for Saint John, begins in a place of darkness and discomfort, as the mystic explains when he interprets the first stanza of his poem:

Once in the dark of night
when love burned bright with yearning, I arose
(O windfall of delight!)

and how I left none knows—
dead to the world my house in deep repose.

The dark night, according to Saint John, comes in two forms—the "night of sense" and the "night of the spirit." These mystical events are both related to the mind and soul, and they are the consequence of contemplation, prayer, solitude, and struggle. The first event, the night of sense, is experienced as privation and death, as a difficult and painful process of purgation. Just when we think our lives are on solid footing, "God turns all this light of theirs into darkness," Saint John writes in his commentary on the poem's first verse. Our certitude collapses into ambiguity; our self-confidence slides into self-doubt. From the divine standpoint, our spiritual growth requires that God step back, withdraw, "hide" from us, and allow us to walk on our own. It is a disorienting and frightening experience. We feel abandoned and forsaken. Yet God is acting out of love.

God places our souls into this dark night, according to Saint John, in order to wean us away from our attachments to the world, to purify us before we continue on our spiritual journey. The night of sense is a night of purification, of mental and emotional anguish. Many of us never move past this trial—our pain feels unbearable and our sense of God's absence too acute. "That which this anguished soul feels most deeply," writes Saint John, "is the conviction that God has abandoned it, that He has cast it away into darkness as an abominable thing." But if we are able to endure this harrowing rite of passage, what at first seemed like divine concealment or detachment can lead us to the second type of night, the "night of the spirit." Saint John explains that

> although this happy night brings darkness to the spirit, it does so
> only to give it light in everything; although it humbles it and makes it
> miserable, it does so only to exalt it and to raise it up; and, although
> it impoverishes it and empties it of all natural affection and attach-
> ment, it does so only that it may enable it to stretch forth, divinely.

The purgation of our senses leads to the emptying of our mind and soul, to a state of openness and receptivity that makes room for the presence of God to dwell within us, for "the light which is to be given to it is a Divine light of the highest kind, which transcends all natural light, and which by nature can find no place in the understanding." In the terrifying void where human faculties and capacities are rendered useless, Saint John discovers the divine presence and experiences spiritual transformation. The same dark night that assaults, confounds, and disintegrates his soul now reintegrates it in a new form, illuminated by the light of divine knowledge that no human intellect can fathom. If God has been absent or hidden from the mystic's life, it was only to redeem it.

Constant faith, even for those who believe in God, is difficult to maintain. When bad things happen to good people, when injustice and evil plague our societies, we often feel that God is far away, that God has abandoned us to an indifferent or hostile universe. But God has not. While there are times that God feels as close as a whisper, there are other times when God withdraws. In Jewish mysticism, this is called *tzimtzum*, or "contraction." When God created the world, according to this idea, God needed to first step back from it so that the earth and its creatures would not drown in an ocean of divine omnipresence. What we view as God's distance can be, in truth, just the opposite. What seems to us like indifference or anger can be, to God, an expression of love, a way of letting history unfold, of preserving human freedom, of giving us room to breathe.

FIRE AND ICE

Psalm 22 begins with an outburst of doubt and despair: "My God, my God, why have You abandoned me?" It ends, however, with a declaration of confidence and praise. There are similar ways to understand some of the mystical interpretations of *hester panim*, God's hiddenness. In either case, it is possible to claim that our experiences of alienation from and abandonment by God will eventually lead to reconciliation, even redemption. Yet many other thinkers and writers do not believe that such an optimistic position is warranted or realistic. They suggest, instead, that our feelings of separation and distance from the divine are too profound, too injurious, and too long-lasting.

One response to this existential reality is confusion. In his play *Waiting for Godot*, Samuel Beckett captures the perplexing, elusive, and at times comic nature of our relationship with transcendence. Like most of his plays and novels, *Waiting for Godot* contains potent yet obscure symbolism, and it lends itself to many interpretations: one of them is that "Godot" represents transcendent reality, a higher power, God. From the first lines of the play to the very last, the mysterious Godot remains invisible and "hidden" from the main characters, Estragon and Vladimir. Yet Godot is the force/entity/reality that propels their actions—and, often, *in*actions.

Near the beginning of the play, Vladimir ruminates about the two thieves who were crucified alongside Jesus and how odd it is that only one of the four evangelists mentions a thief being saved. Following a philosophical and comical exchange between the two men, Estragon suddenly says that they need to leave. Vladimir disagrees and reminds Estragon that they are "waiting for Godot." The men cannot decide whether they are in the right place, but they think that they are supposed to wait beside the tree that is situated, leafless and forlorn, next to them.

Apart from the tree (of knowledge?), Vladimir and Estragon stand alone on the barren stage. To their puzzlement and dismay, Godot is nowhere to be found:

> ESTRAGON: He should be here.
> VLADIMIR: He didn't say for sure he'd come.
> ESTRAGON: And if he doesn't come?
> VLADIMIR: We'll come back tomorrow.
> ESTRAGON: And then the day after tomorrow.
> VLADIMIR: Possibly.
> ESTRAGON: And so on.
> VLADIMIR: The point is—
> ESTRAGON: Until he comes.
> VLADIMIR: You're merciless.

Godot never arrives. Still, Estragon and Vladimir insist on waiting for him. Is their behavior an expression of commitment and faith, or an exercise in pointlessness and absurdity? If the two men represent humanity, and Godot represents God, then Beckett seems to be implying that a great gulf separates one from the other. "Godot" is a name, an aspiration, a force that drives the actions and fuels the passions of Estragon and Vladimir. How can a figure so distant and detached exert so much influence over events? How can someone—or something—so intangible and absent be so powerful?

It isn't clear how or why Godot plays such a central role in the lives of the men, nor what it is exactly that they are waiting for, other than Godot's presence. Early in the first act, however, this exchange between Vladimir and Estragon offers a clue:

VLADIMIR: Let's wait till we know exactly how we stand.
ESTRAGON: On the other hand it might be better to strike the iron before it freezes.
VLADIMIR: I'm curious to hear what he has to offer. Then we'll take it or leave it.
ESTRAGON: What exactly did we ask him for?
VLADIMIR: Were you not there?
ESTRAGON: I can't have been listening.
VLADIMIR: Oh . . . nothing very definite.
ESTRAGON: A kind of prayer.
VLADIMIR: Precisely.
ESTRAGON: A vague supplication.
VLADIMIR: Exactly.

What they hope for (or hope to express) is vague and indefinite: a "prayer" or a "supplication." Godot seems to have something, or to be something, that the men yearn for and aspire to. Is their goal simply a *connection*, a way of bridging the chasm that separates them from Godot? At the end of the play, Estragon and Vladimir conclude that the only solution to their perplexing and circular predicament is to hang themselves on the tree. But before they can make a noose with the cord that holds up Estragon's pants, it breaks. The men resolve to get a stronger rope with which to hang themselves the next day—that is, Vladimir interjects, "unless Godot comes."

For Beckett, the border between comedy and tragedy is very porous.

Through his novels, stories, and shorter works, Franz Kafka (1883–1924) confronts the themes of distance and inaccessibility with an intensity (and, often, a surrealism) that is similar to Beckett's. In "The Coming of the Messiah," Kafka describes a Messiah who, like the figure of Godot, is absent or hidden from the world:

> The Messiah will come as soon as the most unbridled individual-ism of faith becomes possible—when there is no one to destroy this possibility and no one to suffer its destruction; hence the graves will open themselves.... The Messiah will come only when he is no lon-ger necessary; he will come only on the day after his arrival; he will come, not on the last day, but on the very last.

From the Talmud to Hasidism, rabbis and Jewish thinkers have long argued that human actions can "hasten" the coming of the Messiah. In this vignette, Kafka claims just the opposite: we should wait for the Messiah without regard to the Messiah's actual arrival. Only when we have taken absolute responsibility for our actions, as well as for our own redemp-tion, will the Messiah emerge. At that point, we will no longer need him. Kafka's vision of the Messiah—one in which the Messiah's purpose is not to redeem humanity, but to affirm that we have become *ready* to be redeemed—makes the messianic figure invisible, a being or an entity that is, in the end, detached and irrelevant.

In "Before the Law," Kafka writes about the remoteness and hidden nature, not of a person, but of the Law. In the story, a man from the country seeks to encounter "the Law," but when he reaches the open doorway that leads to the Law, the man is confronted by a doorkeeper who denies him entry. The man asks if he will be permitted access at a later time, to which the doorkeeper responds, "It is possible, but not at this moment." The man bends down to peer through the open door. The doorkeeper laughs: "If you are so strongly tempted, try to get in without my permission. But note that I am powerful. And I am only the lowest doorkeeper. From hall to hall keepers stand at every door, one more powerful than the other. Even the third of these has an aspect that even I cannot bear to look at."

The man faces a challenge that seems Sisyphean: a maze of doors and guards separate him from the Law, and if he tries to advance, he does so at his peril. The system of barriers hides the Law, but it also hinders the man from accessing the Law. The distance between the two is profound, and it appears that there is no way to cross the divide. But the man is determined. He waits by the door for many years, bribing the doorkeeper with all he has. The guard accepts the bribes, but he informs the man that he takes them "only to keep you from feeling that you have left something undone."

When the man—still waiting—is near death, he discerns something in the darkness, "a radiance that streams immortally from the door of the Law." This (divine?) radiance is as close as the man will ever come to a direct encounter with the Law, which remains hidden and inaccessible behind a labyrinth of obstacles. With his dying breath, he asks the doorkeeper a question that has perplexed him over the years: Why, even though everyone seeks the Law, has no one else tried to gain admittance through the door in front of him? The doorkeeper replies, "No one but you could gain admittance through this door, since this door was intended only for you. I am now going to shut it."

Kafka's cryptic parable, like the concept of *hester panim* and the expression of forsakenness in Psalm 22, captures the distance and alienation from transcendent reality that many of us feel. Whether we call it "the Law," "Godot," or "God," that reality can animate and guide our lives even as it simultaneously alienates and bewilders us. While it is elusive, concealed, and (by definition) beyond us, transcendence is something that most of us crave with all of our hearts and souls. Does the gatekeeper in Kafka's story represent our own fears, doubts, and confusion in the face of God's hiddenness? Is his role to punish us, or to protect us? Is the Law, like Godot, an inaccessible, unfathomable reality that we never truly encounter but that we can never give up striving for?

All we are left with is more questions.

One response to our awareness of the transcendent is confusion and a sense of hopelessness. Another is anger. Once we become conscious of our flawed and imperfect nature, how can we *not* at times feel a sense of outrage when forced to face the eternal perfection that God represents? How can finite beings ever live up to the ideal of the infinite? The gulf between the two is too vast. In *The Temple of the Golden Pavilion*, a disturbing novel by the Japanese writer Yukio Mishima (1925–70), the protagonist, Mizoguchi, expresses that rage in radical ways. Mizoguchi is a young Buddhist priest who is afflicted with an ugly face and a terrible stutter. The novel is, fundamentally, about the acolyte's obsession with beauty and his intensifying urge to destroy it.

For Mizoguchi, beauty, in all its transcendent, eternal glory, is embodied by the Temple of the Golden Pavilion (an actual temple in Kyoto that was burned to the ground by a deranged arsonist in 1950). Throughout his childhood, Mizoguchi's father had told him that the Golden Pavilion was the most beautiful building in the world, and over the years Mizoguchi has kept the idea of the temple as a fixture in his imagination and a preoccupation of his mind. Born into a poor household, the ugly and stammering Mizoguchi has no friends at school, and he takes refuge in vengeful fantasies. Once he begins his studies in Kyoto, Mizoguchi's wish to see the temple razed escalates.

The Golden Pavilion, in Mizoguchi's troubled mind, is everything he is *not*: beautiful, perfect, eternal. When he sees it for the first time, the distance between the two is suffocating to him—he feels swallowed by, and imprisoned in, its presence:

> The Golden Temple, which sometimes seemed to be so utterly indifferent to me and to tower into the air outside myself, had now completely engulfed me and had allowed me to be situated within its structure.... How could I possibly stretch out my hands towards life when I was being thus enwrapped in beauty? Perhaps beauty also had the right to demand that I relinquish my earlier aim. For clearly it is impossible to touch eternity with one hand and life with the other.

In Mizoguchi's eyes, the transcendent beauty that the temple represents is unattainable. So, too, is the possibility of coexistence between himself and the Golden Pavilion: How could something so majestic and beautiful exist at the same time as someone so flawed and hideous? The sight of the temple is intolerable to Mizoguchi, and his rage grows, as does his desire to burn the structure down with his own hands.

Mizoguchi discusses his thoughts with his only friend, Kashiwagi, a fellow student who shares a defect (clubbed feet) and a similarly hostile attitude toward beauty. In one of their conversations, Kashiwagi says that

although beauty may give itself to everyone, it does not actually belong to anybody. Let me see. How shall I put it? Beauty—yes, beauty is like a decayed tooth. It rubs against one's tongue, it hangs there, hurting one, insisting on its own existence. Finally it gets so that one cannot stand the pain and one goes to the dentist to have the tooth extracted.

While Kashiwagi's philosophizing does not lead to action on his part, his words incite Mizoguchi even further toward his goal of destroying the temple. At one point, Mizoguchi follows a student and projects his own violent ideas onto him:

I do not know why, but I was convinced that the student was moving step by step toward arson.... In front of him lay fire and destruction; behind was the world of order that he had abandoned.... His black serge back, on which the sun shone down, was full of unhappiness and anger.... I had no doubt that he was being impelled to commit the same act as myself because of the same loneliness, the same unhappiness, the same confused thoughts about beauty. As I followed him, I began to feel that I was witnessing my own deed in anticipation.

The student does not turn out to be an arsonist, but Mizoguchi's projection says a great deal about his own motivations for action; it also proves prescient. Driven by rage, loneliness, confusion, and feelings of distance and detachment, Mizoguchi sets fire to the Golden Pavilion. Just before he lights his first match, Mizoguchi recalls a teaching from the Zen work *Rinzai Roku*: "When ye meet the Buddha, kill the Buddha! . . . Only thus will you escape the trammels of material things and become free."

As he watches the flames from the temple illuminate the night, Mizoguchi has only one thought, and it is the very last line of the novel: "I wanted to live."

Can the infinite and the finite exist at the same time? Is it possible to somehow bridge the gap? If the eternal "otherness" of divine reality makes God remote and inaccessible, even hidden, to human beings, how can we ever hope to forge a meaningful relationship? For some, the answer is that we can't. Two examples of "darker" reactions to this existential dilemma, as we have seen, are confusion and anger. But there are a number of others: we can feel forsaken, abandoned, alone, afraid, even abused.

More often than we'd like to think, however, our feeling of being cut off and isolated is a result of our own choices and behavior. When we sin, when we distance ourselves from the divine through our illicit actions, it may appear that God has turned God's back to us. But God hasn't. *We* have caused the separation, and *we* are responsible for our feelings of isolation. Even when we are able to experience God through solitary experiences (as I have for many years), we limit ourselves. As I highlighted at the start of this chapter, my relationship with a former congregant helped to show me that there are other paths to the divine, interpersonal and communal ones. When we reach out beyond ourselves and see the godly in others, when we view other people as assets rather than threats to our spiritual journey, we discover a new portal to God, and we grow.

We are not alone, and even when we start to feel lonely and isolated, there is a way out. If we are ready and receptive, if we are sufficiently evolved to treat our feeling of separation from God as impermanent and as an opportunity for inner transformation, then our dark night of the soul can lead to reconciliation and renewal. A fissure between God and humanity—an experience of divine hiddenness—does not have to turn into a permanent condition or a cause for confusion, despair, or rage.

It can, instead, become our path to repair, our catalyst for communion.

7

Return, Repair, Repent

A FEW MONTHS AFTER MY position as senior rabbi ended, I had time on my hands. While I had some teaching and consulting gigs, I hadn't yet decided what I wanted to do next in my professional career. My wife was teaching at a private school in Manhattan and was supportive of my using the time to get away and do more focused thinking. I wanted to combine work in the Jewish world with an experience in a far-flung destination, and after a few false starts, I created a six-week engagement with a small synagogue in Dunedin, New Zealand, a city in the Otago Region of the South Island.

In terms of geography, Dunedin was about as far away from New York City as I could possibly get. At the time, that didn't play a conscious role in my decision, but now that I have some distance from that period in my life, I think that it did probably figure into it. I was not doing an especially good job of being a husband; I was more concerned with finding my next position than I was with spending quality time with my wife. And my connection to the Jewish community was superficial and tenuous: unless I was hired to give a talk or lead a service, I generally did not attend synagogue or light a Sabbath candle.

I felt disengaged from everything around me, personally and professionally. For me, New Zealand was an attempt to shake off that numbness as much as it was a place to return to, or rediscover, myself.

When I wasn't working with members of the synagogue in Dunedin, a congregation that began with the Central Otago gold rush in the 1860s, I could do as I pleased. My location allowed me easy access to many of the South Island's fjords, glaciers, rain forests, and mountains. My original plan to walk the famous Milford Track in Fiordlands National Park was thwarted by torrential rains that washed out most of the major trails in the area. After that disappointment, however, I was able to explore by foot the fantastical region around Mount Cook, go wreck diving in the Marlborough Sound, and go skydiving near Queenstown. I took two weeks and made a loop around much of the South Island, where I went on several other spectacular hikes as well.

My life back in New York felt very distant. That was telling in itself. Midway through my experience in New Zealand, the city I had known for two decades seemed like a memory of youth, and the marriage I had been in for the past five years felt strangely unreal. I wasn't happy, and staying in our marital status quo wasn't fair to either of us. In my heart, I knew what had to happen, for both of our sakes—and I'd known it for some time. Up to that point, though, I'd lacked the courage to follow my gut, to concede that our union was not working and that we needed to get a divorce. My numbness had crippled my ability not only to feel, but to act.

During my drive around the South Island, I spent three nights in Picton, a small harbor town and site of the terminal for the ferry that connects the South Island with the North Island across Cook Strait. I was in Picton over a weekend, and because I was traveling though New Zealand out of the main holiday season, there were virtually no tourists on the streets or in the pubs. I met a number of locals in town: a retired navy diver and scuba shop owner; a former parole officer who was in between jobs; a college graduate with no plans for the future and no cares in the world.

That Saturday night, I drank with a group of young Maori women. They were excited to meet an American, and when they found out that I'd played rugby for several years (New Zealand was preparing to host the Rugby World Cup at the time), they refused to let me pay for my drinks. After teasing me for not having any tattoos, they invited me and some others to join them at one of their homes outside of town to continue our little party. I felt comfortable with these total strangers. There was no pretense, no flirtation, no hidden motives—just a group of men and women eating and drinking and laughing through the early morning hours. I walked down a hill back toward Picton, occasionally stumbling, intermittently lost, and free. I felt no constraints, no commitments.

But at least I felt something. I did not exactly feel happy, and I did not feel that I had found peace; my restlessness remained. But I did feel that I had returned to, or regained, a part of myself that had been missing for some time. I was well acquainted with the night, and its familiarity—whatever its lures and traps—felt like a homecoming of sorts. Maybe I was meant to be alone, I told myself. Maybe it took a journey to New Zealand, to the geographical periphery, to rediscover my passion. It may have been an immature passion, but it was a passion nonetheless. For freedom.

I returned to New York City less numb, but even more disengaged from my life there. Staying in my marriage felt like living a lie. When my wife and I did things that couples do, like shopping at the supermarket or having dinner at a restaurant, I felt as if I were harboring a terrible secret from her. I couldn't go through the motions anymore. One night, after a very difficult and sad conversation, I explained that we needed to get a divorce. I'd never experienced such a feeling of sorrow before, or such a sense of failure. We just couldn't make each other happy. Had we wasted our last five years?

I knew that I would be an outlier once more. I'd be free, but I did not have clarity about what would happen next in my life or my career. I did not know if I would be alone forever or if I would ever take another job as a rabbi.

Yet I could feel again. I could feel again for the first time in years.

"How shall we return?" (Malachi 3:7)

Malachi is the final book in the prophetic section (Nevi'im) of the Hebrew Bible, and Malachi himself is the last of the twelve minor prophets whose lives and words are found there. But who was this figure? Malachi's name does not appear anywhere else in the Bible. For that reason, as well as because his name in Hebrew means "My messenger," some scholars have claimed that Malachi is not a proper, personal name at all, but an anonymous designation for the author (which would make the book unique in this biblical section). Most scholars agree that the book of Malachi was likely written at some point during the Persian period, after the restoration and reconsecration of the Second Temple in Jerusalem, in 516 BCE.

Malachi is divided into six distinct units that are often referred to as disputations or "questionings" between God and the people of Israel. A number of scholars have suggested that the book as a whole is structured along the lines of a judicial trial, a suzerain treaty, or a discussion of a covenant that has been broken. The problem areas that are underscored include love, honor, infidelity, justice, and speaking against God. The nature and magnitude of the disputations indicate that the relationship between God and Israel has suffered grave damage, and that the rupture must be repaired.

After God reminds the Israelites that the bond between them, while damaged, has not been destroyed, God says, "Return to Me, and I will return to you." In the same verse, Israel responds with a terse, two-word question: *bameh nashuv*, or "How shall we return?" (Mal. 3:7). Is this question asked in the spirit of deference, or in defiance? Is it an expression of sarcasm, or a heartfelt and humble inquiry about finding a path to overcome their estrangement and repair their wounded relationship? The answer is not clear. What is clear is that *teshuvah*, an act of return or repentance, is their only hope.

A BRIDGE TO RECONNECTION

Many Jews associate the concept of *teshuvah* with the Days of Awe, a period that is also known as the Ten Days of Repentance. It is the time of year when we are compelled to turn inward, when our everyday concerns and distractions are suspended so that we may focus exclusively on matters of moral character and the soul. If we have sinned, as all of us inevitably have, then the Days of Awe become our season for atonement, a time to ask God, and those we have wronged, to forgive us.

For most serious Jewish (and non-Jewish) thinkers, the opportunities for *teshuvah* are not so limited, nor are its descriptions so narrow. Maimonides writes extensively about *teshuvah* in his great code, the *Mishneh Torah*. In a section titled "The Laws of Repentance," he explains his conception of authentic *teshuvah*:

> Perfect repentance occurs when an opportunity presents itself to the offender for repeating the offense and he refrains from committing it because of his repentance and not out of fear or physical inability.

If, however, one repents only in his old age, when he is no longer able to do what he used to do, his repentance, although not the best, will, nevertheless, do him some good. Even if a person transgressed all his life and repented on the day of his death and died during his repentance, all his sins are pardoned.

Maimonides addresses the topic of *teshuvah* with both common sense and his hallmark rationalism (which aligns with the fact that the *Mishneh Torah* was written as a practical guide for Jewish behavior and belief). Perfect repentance, or *teshuvah gemurah*, is something that must be demonstrated, to oneself and to others. And it has two prerequisites: first, the penitent must resist the temptation to repeat the original offense when a new opportunity to commit it emerges; second, the desire to refrain from the sin must derive from repentance itself, not from fear of punishment or the inability to perform it again. While the act of *teshuvah* is observable, the impetus behind it is not. Perfect repentance is the result of inner contrition, not external pressure.

For Maimonides, there are different levels of *teshuvah*. If a person does not repent until well into old age, when that person lacks the will or ability to commit the transgressions of his or her youth, repentance will still be of enormous benefit (although it will not be *teshuvah* of the most meritorious type). Even if a person has lived a lifetime of sin and does not repent until the day of his or her death, that final act of *teshuvah* will still be accepted, and that individual's sins will all be completely forgiven.

The importance of repentance is not limited only to outward acts:

> Just as a man must repent of these, so must he scan and search his evil traits, repenting of anger, hatred, envy, scoffing, greed, vainglory, etc. One must repent of all these failings. They are worse than sinful acts. When a person is addicted to them, he finds it difficult to eliminate them.

God's vision encompasses internal attitude and intention as well as external behavior. God's jurisdiction, therefore, extends beyond merely the behavioral and social dimensions of human life—it reaches into our soul. We are responsible for *all* of our sins, whether they relate to outer action or they occur deep in our heart. In Maimonides's thought, these latter, "invisible" transgressions are the most severe and difficult to expunge from our characters. Society cannot and will not punish us for being greedy, hateful, or arrogant. Our impulse to repent of these inward sins must have its source in our moral conscience, a conscience that God has implanted in us all.

Maimonides approaches the issue of *teshuvah* as a *moral* virtue, a quality and an action that relates to both behavior and character. For Rabbi Yechiel ben Yekutiel, a thirteenth-century Italian thinker who wrote *Sefer Ma'alot ha-Midot* (The book of virtues and values), *teshuvah* relates to *spirituality* as much as to morality. And it holds a place in his spiritual worldview just as lofty as it does in the thinking of Malachi and Maimonides. *Teshuvah* is a virtue so unique it is coeternal with God:

> Know, my students, that the virtue of teshuvah is very great. Because of its importance, the Holy One made it precede the creation of the world. As it is written, "Before the mountains came into being, before You brought forth the earth and the world, from eternity to eternity, You are God." (Ps. 90:2) And right after that verse it is written: "You return [*tashev*] man to [contrition], and You decreed, 'Return you mortals!'" (Ps. 90:3) And not only that, but this [virtue] touches the throne of glory, as it is written: "Return [*shuvah*], O Israel, to the Lord your God." (Hosea 14:2)

Using Psalm 90 as a proof text, Yechiel claims that God made *teshuvah* precede the creation of the world. If this is the case, then *teshuvah* represents a virtue that transcends time and space; it is an eternal virtue, or value, rather than one that is context specific. And *teshuvah* is as much about the idea of "return" as it is about repentance. It is the path by which we can reunite with our Creator, our true source.

Teshuvah has the power to bring us to God's "throne of glory" as well. In Merkavah mysticism, one of the earliest Jewish mystical circles, there are frequent descriptions of "visions of the throne"—encounters between mystics and the Godhead. While Yechiel does not claim to have had such an experience himself, his mystical impulses surface very clearly when he discusses *teshuvah*. For example, Yechiel notes that even if a person merely "thinks in his heart" of performing *teshuvah*, the latent spiritual energy of the virtue will instantly ascend to the highest heaven. The mere *inclination* to repent/return catalyzes the elevation of our spiritual desires and aspirations. *Teshuvah*'s power is immediate and everlasting; its scope is cosmic.

Despite his mystical leanings, Yechiel does share some similarities with Maimonides, an arch-rationalist. He writes that even if a person was completely evil all his life but then performed true *teshuvah*, "at the end of his days the Holy One does not remind him of any of his transgressions that he committed in the beginning." One of the greatest benefits of *teshuvah* to the person who returns/repents is its unique ability not only to counteract past misdeeds, but to *nullify* them. Like Maimonides, Yechiel claims that even after a lifetime of transgression and wickedness, if a person commits a final act of *teshuvah*, it will be accepted without reservation by God, all his or her sins will be forgiven, and that person's moral slate will be wiped clean.

Sinful people—namely, all human beings—possess souls that are, or that can often become, sick. *Teshuvah*, however, has the power to heal them:

And you must know, my students, that teshuvah is medication for sins and iniquities, just as bandages and other sorts of medications will heal wounds and injuries. And not only that, but also through teshuvah a person will become beloved to the Holy One where once the Holy One despised him because he pursued the desires of his heart and his eyes and went after his evil inclinations.

Teshuvah is spiritual medicine. Anyone who commits an act of sin has a sick soul in dire need of healing. Just as medications and bandages help to mend an unhealthy body, so does *teshuvah* heal an unhealthy soul. Yet *teshuvah* does more than mend the soul. It also repairs the damaged relationship between the sinner and God. While God may "despise" the person who embraces lustfulness and excess, the *ba'al teshuvah*—the person who turns back/returns to God—can bring about *tikkun*, or spiritual mending, and once again become one of God's most treasured and "beloved" creations.

In Malachi 3:7, God implores the Israelites to "return to Me, and I will return to you." Their reply, as we have noted, is a question: "How shall we return?" There is no single path to achieve that objective. The concept of *teshuvah* in Judaism involves three distinct yet interrelated experiences: return, repair, and repentance. All of them are necessary, in different ways and at different times, to heal our souls and mend our broken relationship with God. In this sense, *teshuvah* is also *restorative*, an experience that rebalances the psycho-spiritual equilibrium that sin disrupts. *Teshuvah* restores the soul to its original self and renews the covenant between God and humankind.

When we sin, according to an idea in Hasidic thought, there remains in our soul a point of purity, a divine spark that is never extinguished. While we may become distant from God, God stays close to us. But how, after sin shatters our moral and spiritual balance, do we return our soul to the primal unity of existence, to that place of wholeness where the relationship between humanity and God is seamless and true?

Psychological thinkers acknowledge the universal human longing to return to what William James (1842–1910) calls "the unity of the self." To put it in Jungian terms, every human being possesses an impulse to integrate all the forces of his or her soul, particularly when they have been torn asunder by negative actions and attitudes. To do this, the self must resolve its inner contradictions and conflicts and impose an internal unity. Reason, willpower, and social pressure are tools that psychology has often argued would bring about wholeness and equanimity (*sh'lemut* in Hebrew).

Religion, on the other hand, claims that such integration is not possible without the presence and help of God. *Sh'lemut* is a state in which the soul has reached a place of unity, harmony, and integration with itself, and for mystical thinkers especially it is viewed as an experience that connects us, or reconnects us, with God. In the thought of some mystical thinkers, that link is related to *teshuvah*.

Rabbi Abraham Isaac Kook (1865–1935) was the first Ashkenazic chief rabbi of Mandatory Palestine, a mystic, and one of the most celebrated rabbis of the twentieth century. In *The Lights of Penitence*, Rav Kook (as he is widely known) addresses the topic of *teshuvah* in a comprehensive and unique way. For him, *teshuvah* is not a question of ethics versus spirituality, but a dialectic of ethics *and* spirituality. Rav Kook explores the impact of *teshuvah* on the totality of the human being, and he advances a mystical approach that views it is as a reintegration, reunion, or "homecoming" with God: "*Teshuvah* is fundamentally a movement of return to originality, to the source of life and highest being in their wholeness." Rav Kook expounds on this idea:

> When we forget the essence of our soul itself, when we are distracted from introspection, from the content of inner life, everything becomes confused and doubtful. The beginning of repentance which immediately illumines the darkness is that man return to himself, to the root of his soul, and he will at once return to God, to the soul of all souls, and will stride ever higher in holiness and purity. This is true for the individual and for the entire nation, for all of humanity, for the perfection of existence as a whole; its ruin always comes when it forgets itself.

Through *teshuvah*, all distinctions between the self and God dissolve; when we return to the origin or root of our souls, we return to God, "the soul of all souls." *Teshuvah* is not possible *without* God, and yet, paradoxically, it also leads *to* God. For Rav Kook—a Jewish thinker who saw the divine as equally present in labor Zionists as in Talmudic sages—the power of *teshuvah* is accessible not only to individual Jews, but to the community and nation, as well as to all of humanity. If we "forget" our true source and root (i.e., God), we become confused, doubtful, lost. Our redemption from darkness, our (and the world's) *repair*, comes through reconnection with divinity.

While *teshuvah* engenders unity and a state of *sh'lemut*, sin causes division and disunion between human beings and God. Our struggle between these two forces is one that is challenging and lifelong. Repentance and sin are interwoven aspects of human existence. *Teshuvah* is part of the essence of reality itself, but so is sin:

Repentance preceded the world and is thus a fundament of the world. Life becomes complete as its essential nature is revealed. And because nature, in and of itself, does not have the property of seeing and distinguishing [i.e., it has no freedom of choice], sin dominates, "for there is not one good man on earth who does what is best and doesn't err." (Eccles. 7:20) Vitiating the naturalness of life to keep man free of sin, that in itself is the gravest sin, "and make expiation on his behalf for the guilt that he incurred through the corpse." (Num. 6:11) Thus repentance repairs the damage and returns the world and life to its source, precisely by revealing the highest fundament of their essence, the world of freedom, and hence we call the name of the Lord "the living God."

In Rav Kook's mystical thought, *teshuvah* is a divine virtue that preceded the world and served as a foundation *of* the world. Yet while *teshuvah* leads to self-integration, self-awareness, and the liberation of our soul, sin, as an act of division, constricts and enslaves our soul, obscuring the divine spark within it. We are presented with a paradox: sin is a real, even necessary, feature of the human condition (it is what *makes* us human), but we cannot be truly free or alive—we cannot live in a state of unity with God—until we have broken the shackles of sin. *Teshuvah* bridges the divide, aligns our soul with its source, and returns us and the world to a place of wholeness.

WINE-DARK SEAS, VERNAL WOODS, AND FLAMING OCEANS

Irrespective of whether *teshuvah* is discussed in moral, spiritual, or mystical terms, its value to our lives is beyond dispute. When the Israelites ask God, "How shall we return?," they demonstrate confusion (or skepticism) about discerning a way back to God after having fallen away. And if God is, as Rav Kook claims, the point of origin for the human soul, then *teshuvah* represents our soul's home and safe harbor after a voyage through the reefs, shoals, and tumult of sin and conflict. But how "safe" is the journey home? Can introspection, contrition, and reconnection be considered "heroic"?

The theme of return, and the challenges associated with it, play a major role in Western mythology and literature. In *The Hero with a Thousand Faces*, Joseph Campbell (1904–87) introduces his theory of the "monomyth," the idea that most of the world's important myths share a fundamental structure. Campbell argues that three basic elements of that structure—separation, initiation, and return—are usually present in narratives that present us with heroic figures, individuals who are called to great adventures, experience struggle and adversity, and then return to their homes (or to themselves) with new insight, knowledge, and wisdom. Some examples of these archetypal figures are Osiris, Prometheus, the Buddha, Moses, and Jesus.

Odysseus is another. Homer's epic poem the *Odyssey* takes place in the aftermath of the Trojan War (which Homer describes in great detail in the *Iliad*). The poem centers on Odysseus, a Greek soldier and hero, and his journey home across "the wine-dark sea" after the fall and sacking of Troy. Odysseus has been away from his home, the port city of Ithaca, for ten years, and it takes him another ten years to return. Is his journey a form of penance for the death and destruction he has left behind?

During his decade at sea, Odysseus faces many challenges and obstacles. While he surmounts them all, he nevertheless commits more transgressions in the process. Odysseus is a man whose soul is flawed, tortured, and oftentimes lost. Here is Robert Fagles's translation of the opening verses of the poem:

> Sing to me of the man, Muse, the man of twists and turns
> driven time and again off course, once he had plundered
> the hallowed heights of Troy.
> Many cities of men he saw and learned their minds,
> many pains he suffered, heartsick in the open sea,
> fighting to save his life and bring his comrades home.

What are the "sins" of Odysseus? In classical Jewish tradition, there are, in descending order of severity, three basic types of sin: *peshah* (willful crime), *averah* (transgression), and *chet* (missing the mark). While the *Odyssey* suggests that the former soldier—a man of "twists and turns"—is guilty of more serious offenses, he repeatedly commits acts of *chet*, both literally and figuratively, during his return journey to Ithaca. Odysseus, at times unintentionally, strays from the straight and narrow and often goes "off course" into morally ambiguous terrain. From a military standpoint, for instance, he is a master of trickery (e.g., the Trojan horse); from a moral perspective, he can also be a master of deceit. Yet when are Odysseus's misdirections tactical, and when are they *misdeeds*, reflective of the loss of a moral (and, at sea, existential) compass?

At the start of his voyage home from Troy, Odysseus and his twelve ships are driven off course by a storm. On the island of the Cyclopes, a monstrous race of one-eyed cannibals, Odysseus is captured by the giant Polyphemus, who proceeds to eat two of his men. Odysseus manages to get Polyphemus drunk and then blinds him, allowing Odysseus and his men to escape. As Odysseus sails away from the island, he reveals his name and hidden identity with a boastful taunt. Enraged, Polyphemus hurls part of a mountain at him and prays to his father, Poseidon, to thwart Odysseus on his journey. As a result of his hubris, Odysseus remains lost, delaying his return home by many years.

Odysseus misses the mark in other ways. Unlike another hero from the Trojan War, Achilles, whose tragic flaw of vainglory defines and ultimately destroys him, Odysseus is far more complicated. While intelligent and cunning, he is also arrogant and licentious, and he frequently shows questionable judgment. Odysseus falls prey to the sorcery of Circe and the wiles of Calypso, harming his men and delaying his journey. Odysseus also falls prey to insatiable curiosity. He yearns to experience the "forbidden knowledge" of the song of the Sirens; while he plugs his ears with beeswax and has his men tie him to the mast of his ship to prevent him from succumbing to the temptation, his desire to hear the seductive song nearly leads to wrecked ships and lost lives.

Despite the character flaws that delay and disorient Odysseus on his voyage home, he eventually returns to Ithaca. Yet his homecoming is far from a joyous occasion, and it does not represent a return to "wholeness": the former hero arrives late, broken, and alone, and he finds great troubles in his household. During his decade-long absence, it was assumed that Odysseus had died, and his wife, Penelope, must now contend with a group of unruly suitors who are vying for her hand in marriage. Odysseus, in disguise, discovers the situation and slaughters the suitors. Penelope at first cannot believe that her husband has returned, but eventually she reunites with him. Odysseus then reconnects with his family, his land, and his rightful place as king.

Even when we, like Odysseus, are able to return to our home or place of origin, we will never be the same person as we were before we left. Our struggles, triumphs, failures, and (mis?)adventures will inevitably, and irrevocably, transform us. If we are fortunate, we can change in positive, even "heroic" ways—we can grow, learn from our mistakes, evolve into stronger, wiser people. But there is no guarantee. And those we have left behind will change as well. They may even have trouble recognizing us.

Is Odysseus the model of someone who has successfully returned? His character is complex and the answer is not simple. While God may accept our *teshuvah* without reservation or qualification, in the human dimension, return will always be imperfect.

Returning to our home, and to other people, is complicated. As many religious thinkers have argued, returning to God, while difficult, is decidedly *un*complicated: God's capacity to forgive is boundless, and, even if we are at the end of our lives, God will always grant us a blank slate and a fresh start. There are compelling parallels to this idea in the poetry of the Romantic movement of the nineteenth century, generally known as the "Return to Nature." The Romantics have an answer to the question *How shall we return?*: while return in the social context is complex and imperfect, in the context of nature we are provided with the setting, and the inspiration, to experience perfection.

Romanticism was a reaction to (and a revolt against) several forces: the Industrial Revolution, aristocratic social and political norms, and the Enlightenment, particularly its emphasis on reason and the scientific rationalization of nature. The Romantic poets (sometimes referred to as the "nature poets") celebrated emotion, intuition, and simplicity; they extolled farmers and children in their work, and they excoriated the dominance of intellect and the oppressiveness of "philosophy" (largely understood as physical science). William Blake expresses this sentiment in "London":

> In every cry of every Man,
> In every Infant's cry of fear,
> In every voice, in every ban,
> The mind-forg'd manacles I hear.

The "Return to Nature" was an attempt to return to, and restore, the natural state of liberty in human beings. By freeing people from the "mind-forg'd manacles" of reason and science, the Romantics hoped to construct a new, more harmonious world.

While Romanticism was a European phenomenon, it was especially powerful in the imaginations of the English poets. One of the most prominent among them was William Wordsworth (1770–1850). After his disillusionment with the French Revolution, Wordsworth moved to the English countryside and sought the "healing power" of nature. His attitude toward nature changed throughout his life; the subjects of Wordsworth's poems start with animals and sensuality, but his later works have a mystical quality to them. God and nature are one in Wordsworth's poetry. Nature is the all-knowing, all-reaching moral guide and teacher for anyone who is open and receptive to its message:

> One impulse from the vernal wood
> Can teach you more of man,
> Of moral evil and of good
> Than all the sages can. ("The Tables Turned")

Nature is also a protective and reparative force:

> she can so inform
> The mind that is within us, so impress
> With quietness and beauty, and so feed
> With lofty thoughts, that neither evil tongues,

Rash judgments, nor the sneers of selfish men,
Nor greetings where no kindness is, nor all
The dreary intercourse of daily life,
Shall e'er prevail against us, or disturb
Our chearful faith that all which we behold
Is full of blessings. ("Lines Composed a Few Miles above Tintern
    Abbey")

Wordsworth identifies nature with divinity. When we return to nature, we (like those who, in the writings of Rav Kook, experience *teshuvah*) can experience a sense of reconnection, repair, wholeness, harmony. For Wordsworth, nature provides us with our highest pleasure: spiritual communion. Nature is our gateway to a more perfect world:

The breath of this corporeal frame
And even the motion of our human blood
Almost suspended, we are laid asleep
In body, and become a living soul:
While with an eye made quiet by the power
Of harmony, and the deep power of joy,
We see into the life of things. ("Lines Composed a Few Miles above
    Tintern Abbey")

Like Wordsworth, Samuel Taylor Coleridge (1772–1834) became disillusioned with the French Revolution and sought solace in nature. Initially, Coleridge views nature as a purely benevolent power, a spirit that can guide and instruct his own, infant son:

But thou, my babe! shalt wander like a breeze
By lakes and sandy shores, beneath the crags
Of ancient mountain, and beneath the clouds,
Which image in their bulk both lakes and shores
And mountain crags: so shalt thou see and hear
The lovely shapes and sounds intelligible
Of that eternal language, which thy God

Utters, who from eternity doth teach
Himself in all, and all things in himself. ("Frost at Midnight")

Nature, for Coleridge, is not only benevolent, it is also eternal, the meta-physical constant that grounds reality in the face of birth, death, and the vicissitudes of the human journey. How could nature *not* impart wisdom to us? We would be foolish not to enlist its help in teaching future gen-erations of people how to "see and hear" the transcendent Creator who is behind, beneath, and responsible for the works of creation.

Later in his writing career, Coleridge no longer sees nature as purely benevolent, a positive force that generates optimism and leads to unbri-dled joy. In his famous poem "The Rime of the Ancient Mariner," nature plays a central role, but it is one that can become, in the hands of divine providence, punitive and malevolent. At the start of the mariner's tale, he explains to the wedding guest how a powerful storm drove him and his ship down to the South Pole, where he was surrounded by snow and ice. An albatross, viewed by sailors as a good omen, appeared above the mariner and his crew:

> The ice was here, the ice was there,
> The ice was all around:
> It cracked and growled, and roared and howled,
> Like noises in a swound!
>
> At length did cross an Albatross,
> Thorough the fog it came;
> As if it had been a Christian soul,
> We hailed it in God's name.

The mariner confesses how, for no apparent reason, he shot and killed the albatross with a crossbow. As punishment for his brazen and wanton crime, nature itself seems to punish the mariner, along with his crew—as if it is an instrument of God. The ship is blown into tropical waters. The winds die down and the vessel is immobilized on the still and silent ocean. The sun beats down mercilessly on the sailors:

All in a hot and copper sky,
The bloody Sun, at noon,
Right up above the mast did stand,
No bigger than the Moon.

Water, water, every where,
And all the boards did shrink;
Water, water, every where,
Nor any drop to drink.

The mariner and his crew, parched and tortured by the undrinkable ocean water that surrounds their ship, are plagued by nightmarish visions and haunted by horrific dreams. The sky is aflame and the ocean burns:

About, about, in reel and rout
The death-fires danced at night;
The water, like a witch's oils,
Burnt green, and blue and white.

And some in dreams assurèd were
Of the Spirit that plagued us so;
Nine fathom deep he had followed us
From the land of mist and snow.

At first, nature engulfs the ship with ice, snow, and mist. As a result of the mariner's dark act, they must now contend with fire. Is it the avenging spirit of the albatross that pursues them across the seas, or is it God? In either case, nature is the central, and capricious, character of the poem. The mariner's fellow sailors eventually perish, and the mariner returns to his home in England. Like Odysseus, however, he is broken, humbled, and alone. Out of a sense of compulsion (or as penance?), the old mariner must share his "rime" with all who will listen to the end of his days.

The wedding guest is stunned by the mariner's tale. He bids farewell to the old sailor and walks away from their encounter "a sadder and a wiser man."

The concept of *teshuvah*, as we have seen, can take many forms. In the writings of religious thinkers, mystics, and poets, it can be variously understood as repentance, repair, or return. When we act with *teshuvah* toward God, we can experience perfect reconciliation, a return to wholeness and harmony. When we direct our *teshuvah* toward other people, the results can often be incomplete and unpredictable. Even nature, a force that can restore and center us when we have lost our way and yearn to regain it, is sometimes capable of doing great harm to us if we are not respectful and vigilant.

How shall we return? is a question without a single (or clear) answer, but it is a question that usually suggests we are on the wrong path, and that we must, at the risk of life and limb, seek out a new direction on our journey. Even if it makes us sadder and wiser. For me, it took a trip to the South Island of New Zealand to rediscover my passion for freedom—and to find the strength of will to end a marriage that was not working. The divorce that followed was sad and painful, but it put both of us on new paths that, I continue to hope, will lead to more enlightened and fulfilling lives.

In the book of Malachi, *How shall we return?* is a question that is presented in the plural, not the singular. Why? Perhaps to teach us that we are *all* lost, at one time or another, during the course of our lives. Yet while the feeling of being lost can result in confusion, anxiety, and loneliness, it can also catalyze real and necessary growth.

We are not doomed just because we become lost. At the outset of the *Divine Comedy*, Dante, at the midpoint of his life, is aware that he has strayed into a wilderness. Despite his fears, the poet travels through hell, climbs the mountain of purgatory, and gains a vision of celestial paradise. The Torah also shows how a journey through the wilderness can result in transformation and growth. After the ordeal of their bondage in Egypt, the Israelites sojourn through the maze of the Sinai Desert. Yet it is precisely in this desolate environment that God appears to them and reveals the covenant, a pact through which they and their descendants will return to God and be redeemed.

These episodes are not just epic tales; they are metaphors for life. At their core, they are promises that beyond our trials and struggles there is hope, a path out of the wilderness that is tortuous but true. We may not always "return" to the place from which we began our journey, but we can rest assured that we *will* arrive—in a place that offers us a fresh start, renewed perspective, unexpected opportunities, and a new sense of home.

8

Down in the Valley

AS I LOADED UP MY car with clothes, shoes, books, and dog food, my midlife crisis showed no sign of abating. While I still had no clue what my life or career would look like when I returned to Chicago, I had been hired to work for the next four months as a visiting scholar at an interfaith center based at a small university in Virginia. The school, Eastern Mennonite University, was in the heart of the Shenandoah Valley, a rural area of great beauty that had once served as the breadbasket of the Confederacy. I looked forward to the change of scenery. On good days, I felt as if my life was in a state of limbo that never quite seemed to lift. On bad days, I felt like I'd hit a dead end.

I gave myself two days to make the seven-hundred-mile road trip to Bridgewater, Virginia, where I'd be staying. I packed enough items to carry me through the semester, and when I'd finished, I led Jake, my Border Collie–German Shepherd mix, into the back seat. It was freezing; I was leaving in early January, just a couple of days after New Year's, and Chicago was in the grip of another cold spell. The roads were icy, and I didn't have much confidence in my fourteen-year-old vehicle. But we pushed off after breakfast.

There's not much to say about the interstates in Indiana and Ohio, except that they are fast. With little of interest to look at during my drive, I occupied my mind with thoughts about my life. Here I was, in my late forties, divorced and childless. Sure, I'd written a bunch of books and helped to found a synagogue, but when I compared myself to other men my age, I felt like a failure. Most of my friends had homes in the suburbs, wives they'd been married to for many years, and kids getting ready for college. They had stable, well-paying jobs and health insurance. They took regular vacations with their families. And they seemed reasonably happy with their lot in life.

I wasn't. My old behavioral patterns were not leading me toward healthy, intimate relationships. My search for a new career had stalled. If I'd ever had a center, it was not holding. I was on the road, cold and alone, with only a dog for companionship. This limbo had lasted well over three years now, and it was very difficult for me to see light at the end of the tunnel. I beat up on myself and lamented my existential condition for hours, and when we pulled into a pet-friendly motel in Chillicothe, Ohio, I was exhausted. It was a Friday night, the start of the Jewish Sabbath, but I did nothing to celebrate it. I ordered a pizza, walked Jake around town, and went to bed.

The next morning, as I drove through southern Ohio and crossed into West Virginia, the landscape became much more interesting. The hills, while small, broke up the drive's monotony. Tiny, often dilapidated towns squeezed themselves into tight hollows. There was something beautiful, but also faintly menacing, about West Virginia. Maybe it was the haunting appearance of some of the old buildings. Or the way the shadows snaked through the hollows and around the homes. Whatever it was, it was exhilarating. I felt alive. And I began to enjoy the adventure of my journey.

The past few years had given me some *gifts* as well as many challenges. I was about to embark on a semester-long job in academia, one that would allow me to teach an elective I'd always wanted to offer (on spiritual writers and spiritual writing) and that would team me with an Iranian and a Mennonite scholar for a comparative religion course. Prior to that, I had worked as a senior writer at a large public relations firm in Chicago, an experience that gave me a taste of corporate America and the PR/marketing/advertising world, about which I knew very little. It was an experience that was mostly vapid and disturbing, but I learned a great deal about myself as a result. I had adopted a dog I loved, and who was now accompanying me to my rural destination. And, best of all, I'd gotten to spend unexpected quality time with my mother and father, both in their late seventies. More than providing me with a glimpse of alternative career paths, that time with my parents had been a profound experience of reconnection and healing.

The Shenandoah Valley sits between the Allegheny and the Blue Ridge Mountains, and it is stunning. This contrasts starkly with the fact that it was the site of great violence and death during the Civil War. As a consequence of scorched-earth strategies, most of it was burned by troops. Yet when I entered Virginia and drove for a while, and when the Blue Ridge finally came into view, all I could see was the valley's beauty. There was no trace of fire or ferocity. Before me was a tranquil land that filled me with a sense of hopefulness, a place of rebirth and renewal that I had encountered at just the right time. I could go on, even in the face of uncertainty. I had no other choice.

"If a man dies, can he live again?" (Job 14:14)

Within the first two chapters of the biblical book named after him, Job has lost virtually everything—his property, his children, and his health. In chapter 14, after observing that human life is "short-lived and sated with trouble" (Job 14:1), Job notes that even trees possess the capacity to be reborn:

> There is hope for a tree;
> If it is cut down it will renew itself;
> Its shoots will not cease. (Job 14:7)

Yet what about human beings? Can they be reborn and live again? While Judaism itself focuses less on the hereafter than on the here and now, Job's question cannot be ignored.

The present world is referred to in Hebrew as *olam ha-zeh* (this world), and the world that follows, or the afterlife, is called *olam ha-ba* (the world-to-come). These are postbiblical phrases and concepts, however. In the Torah, there are less overt intimations of an afterlife. One of them, an idea that surfaces after the deaths of Abraham, Ishmael, Isaac, Jacob, Aaron, and Moses, is that of being "gathered" to one's people. It is not clear what this expression means. For Rabbi Levi ben Gershon, or Gersonides (1288–1344), it is connected to the soul. While the soul is in the human body, argues Gersonides, it lives in isolation; when it leaves the body at the moment of death, it rejoins its source, and it is gathered back to its original state of "glory."

There is broad consensus on the immortality of the soul in Judaism and the other Abrahamic faith traditions. But agreement on the soul's eternality begs the question of what happens to it after we die. What is the *experience* of the soul in *olam ha-ba*?

BANQUETS, BODIES, AND ANALOGIES

The Torah contains a number of references to Sheol, an abode for the dead. The Hebrew word *sheol*, in the biblical context, is often understood to mean "deep" or "underground." When God punishes the rebellious Korah and his followers in Numbers 16:31–33, for example, the text states that the ground opens up, the rebels descend into Sheol, and they are then swallowed by the earth. In later rabbinic literature, Sheol can have meanings other than underground, such as "grave," "place of waiting," and "place of healing." Sheol, for some rabbis, is not only an abode for the wicked, but a place where all who die, whether righteous or unrighteous, must go. It is a place that is cut off from God, but it is also a place of purification that prepares our souls to meet God.

There are other images and myths that are used to paint a picture of the world-to-come. At the end of the book of Job, in chapters 40 and 41, the mythic beasts Behemoth and Leviathan are described in detail. These primeval creatures are endowed with enormous strength and, in the Bible, represent the forces of darkness and chaos. While humans like Job cannot ever hope to control them, in God's hands both Behemoth and Leviathan are reduced to the status of divine pets, with rings through their noses and Leviathan on a leash. In postbiblical thought, the monsters play a different, more eschatological role, yet one that still underscores God's dominance and control.

Rabbinic legend tells of a great battle that will occur at the end of days between Behemoth and Leviathan. At the close of this apocalyptic battle—the harbinger of the world-to-come—God will slay both of them with a mighty sword. Then, using the skin of Leviathan, God will make sukkot (huts) to shelter the righteous, who will feast on its flesh, along with the flesh of Behemoth (BT Bava Batra 74b–75a). In the mythic imagination, *olam ha-ba* is a heavenly banquet, a place where the soul celebrates the victory of God over the forces of chaos and the triumph of life over death.

This messianic vision and aspiration are expressed liturgically at the end of the festival of Sukkot, also known as *z'man simchateinu,* or the "time of our rejoicing." Upon leaving the sukkah, a person traditionally recites the following prayer:

> May it be Your will, Lord our God and God of our ancestors, that just as I have fulfilled and dwelt in this sukkah, so may I merit in the coming year to dwell in the sukkah of the skin of Leviathan. Next year in Jerusalem.

In a nod to the talmudic myth, this prayer references Leviathan as a symbol of eschatological longing, along with Jerusalem, which (as is the case at the end of the Passover seder) serves as an image for the state of peace and joy that will define the world-to-come. The rabbis conceive of *olam ha-ba* as an extension of *olam ha-zeh,* a place where we can realize our deepest pleasures in eternal and infinite degrees.

While some rabbis picture *olam ha-ba* as a heavenly banquet, others use a different image. In both the Talmud and Jewish mysticism, two types of spiritual abodes are mentioned that are referred to as *gan eden,* or the "Garden of Eden." In the first type, the "lower" *gan eden,* the mythic garden is described as terrestrial in nature, a place of abundance and fertility like that in the second chapter of the book of Genesis. The second type, the "higher" *gan eden,* is envisioned as being celestial in nature, a wholly spiritual reality that is inhabited by righteous souls (be they Jewish or non-Jewish). The sages make a distinction between *gan* (garden) and Eden. They note that Adam lived in the *gan,* while Eden has never been, nor ever will be, witnessed by any mortal eye.

In Jewish eschatology, the higher *gan eden* is often called the "garden of righteousness." It is a spiritual place that has existed since the beginning of the world, and it will appear for all to see in the world-to-come. For the mystics and other early esoteric thinkers, the righteous who dwell there will behold the transcendent sight of the creatures who bear God's celestial throne (an image drawn from Ezekiel's prophetic vision of the divine chariot). The righteous will walk and dance with God, and (according to the apocryphal book of Enoch) they will be "in the light of the sun, and the chosen ones [will be] in the light of eternal life. And there will be no end to the days of their life and the days of the holy ones will be without number" (Enoch 58:3).

The celestial garden of Eden in the world-to-come is a place that is reserved for the righteous. Yet even those souls whose wickedness has driven them far from God, those who have descended into Sheol (or Gehinnom, another Hebrew word for "underworld"), will ultimately be purified and brought into "the light of eternal life."

The mythic and mystical conceptions of the afterlife that I have highlighted stand in stark contrast to the rationalist view of Maimonides. In *The Guide for the Perplexed*, he writes that human beings possess two types of intellect, one that is "material" and one that is "immaterial." The material intellect is dependent on, and influenced by, the body, while the immaterial intellect is independent of corporeality. The latter type of intellect is, in the Scholastic thought of Maimonides, identical with what most of us would call the soul. It is a direct emanation of the "active intellect," the Aristotelean idea of a universal, all-encompassing intelligence that orders and animates existence.

When, through human reason, the immaterial intellect attains correct knowledge of the active intellect (i.e., when our soul reunites with its source, or God) we can achieve a purely spiritual existence. For Gersonides, as I noted earlier, it is death that allows the soul to return to its source; for Maimonides, we can realize an immaterial, spiritual nature while we are still alive. The knowledge of God represents the apex of human striving—it leads to happiness and endows the soul with immortality. At this heightened level of divine consciousness and connection, we are liberated from sin and death. We can taste of *olam ha-ba* even in our mortal, bodily existence.

Bodily existence can viewed as ongoing. Traditional Jewish notions of the world-to-come often include a belief in physical resurrection. In the

Mishnah, belief in the resurrection of the dead is seen as one of Judaism's three essential tenets:

> All Israel have a portion in the world-to-come, for it is written: "Your people, all of them righteous, shall possess the land for all time; they are the shoot that I planted, My handiwork in which I glory." (Is. 60:21) But the following have no portion therein: one who maintains that resurrection is not a biblical doctrine, that the Torah was not divinely revealed, and a heretic. (Sanhedrin 10:1)

Over and above this mishnaic text, Maimonides also lists physical resurrection as one of his thirteen articles of faith. Yet how does Maimonides, an Aristotelian rationalist (and a physician), reconcile the primacy of reason with classical Judaism's assertion that bodily resurrection is a necessary and core Jewish belief? He does it with great caution and nuance. While Maimonides describes the world-to-come in exclusively spiritual terms, and while he posits that those with perfected intellects can experience a taste of *olam ha-ba* in the here and now, he also claims that most of us must wait for death before we can realize a state of divine connection.

Bodily resurrection plays an important role in that process. But Maimonides does not link resurrection with his ideas on the afterlife; instead, he relegates physical resurrection to the status of a future miracle, unrelated to the end of days or the world-to-come. In "The Treatise on Resurrection," Maimonides argues that belief in resurrection is central to Jewish thought and that no sensible person would, or should be permitted to, disagree with its essential truth. He cites the book of Daniel:

> Many of those that sleep in the dust of the earth will awake, some to eternal life, others to reproaches, to everlasting abhorrence. . . . But you, go on to the end; you shall rest, and arise to your destiny at the end of the days. (Dan. 12:2, 12)

Maimonides resolves the apparent contradiction between his two claims—namely, that eternal life is noncorporeal in nature and that bodily resurrection will occur—in a unique way. Maimonides does not argue that resurrection is permanent. Because, in his view, God does not violate the laws of nature, it is through the mediation of angels (often used by Maimonides as metaphors for the principles by which the world functions) that divine interaction occurs. If a unique event such as resurrection takes place, even if we perceive it as a miracle, it is still not a violation of the order of the universe.

If resurrection occurs, it will happen at an indeterminate time before the world-to-come, which is a separate phenomenon and which will be purely spiritual. Any humans who have died and are resurrected will eventually die again. What will life be like for those who are resurrected? Maimonides writes that those who return to their bodies will "eat, drink, copulate, beget, and die after a very long life, like the lives of those who will live in the days of the Messiah." In this way, Maimonides dissociates the idea of resurrection from *olam ha-ba* and its completely spiritual character.

In Maimonides's time, many Jewish thinkers claimed that bodily resurrection and the world-to-come were identical. In that context, denying a permanent and universal resurrection bordered on a denial of normative Jewish doctrine. Maimonides, however, extricates himself from this dilemma by arguing that resurrection has nothing to do with the messianic era (in *olam ha-zeh*) or with the afterlife (*olam ha-ba*); instead, Maimonides writes that resurrection will be the result of a miracle that was predicted in the book of Daniel. At an unknown future time, there will be instances of resurrection, but they will be temporary and they will not relate to the end of days and the world-to-come, a completely spiritual existence that is reserved for the righteous.

Rabbi Abraham Ibn Ezra (1089–1164) describes resurrection in ways that, in part, anticipate and parallel the approach of Maimonides. While not denying the doctrine of resurrection, he couches it within a more rationalistic model. He writes,

> The righteous who died in exile will be resurrected when the Messiah comes, for to them apply the words, "the days of My people shall be as long as the days of a tree." (Is. 65:22) They will then delight themselves with Leviathan, Ziz [the sky monster], and Behemoth and die a second time, only to be resurrected again in the world-to-come, in

which they will neither eat nor drink but instead behold and enjoy the glory of the divine presence. (Commentary on Daniel 12:12)

For Ibn Ezra, only a special category of people—the righteous who died in exile—will be resurrected in the messianic era. As reborn beings, they will partake of the same mythic banquet I described earlier in the chapter, feasting on the flesh of the legendary beasts from the sea and land (as well as from the sky). Yet this will be only a temporary, and inferior, celebration. Like Maimonides, Ibn Ezra writes that the resurrected will experience a *second* death. The eternal life that their souls will "awaken" to in *olam ha-ba* will not involve eating or drinking, but only basking in the glory of the divine presence. It will be purely spiritual in nature.

Ibn Ezra describes the afterlife as a qualitatively different reality from the one that is presented by his rabbinic forbearers. Rather than viewing the world-to-come as an extension of this world (through the image of a banquet and physical activity such as eating and drinking), Ibn Ezra's vision is of an existence that will be experienced exclusively by the soul. Since the world-to-come is not of an earthly character, nothing earthly (like a physical body) may participate in it. The soul alone, which does not and cannot die, will delight for all eternity in the radiance of divine reality. Even if our souls are not "reborn," our *experience* of existence will be fundamentally reshaped.

The idea that humanity can experience a spiritual rather than a physical rebirth predates Maimonides and Ibn Ezra by nearly two millennia. In the Bible, this idea is often conveyed through the image of a valley. In First Samuel, David transcends mortal fear and transforms into a future king when he defeats Goliath in the Valley of Elah. In the book of Ezekiel, the besieged prophet receives a mystical vision of the valley of dry bones, a place where the dead are reborn and rise again. In Psalm 23, the author journeys from the murky desolation of the valley of the shadow of death to a lavish table and an overflowing cup that are prepared for him by a divine hand.

It is rather doubtful that the image of a valley is accidental, and it is reminiscent of a similar mystical idea, that of *yeridah*, or "spiritual descent," that I noted in chapter 2. Through these images and analogies of going down before rising up, of descent before ascent, the Jewish tradition conveys a powerful and metaphorical understanding of the role of rebirth and resurrection in our spiritual lives. It is impossible for us to reach peaks without first sojourning in valleys: Abraham, Joseph, and Moses go "down" to Egypt before their journeys toward the Promised Land; David, Ezekiel, and the Psalmist traverse "low" places before they experience rebirth and renewal.

While it is only following our physical deaths that an eternal experience of spiritual renewal/rebirth/resurrection is possible, religious tradition seems to suggest that a taste of the world-to-come is within the grasp of all of us in the here and now.

THE DEATH OF DEATH

Resurrection—specifically, the resurrection of Jesus—has long been central not only to Christian theology, but to Christian art. At first, owing partly to anti-Christian persecution, the resurrection was depicted only indirectly. In the catacombs of Rome, artists hinted at the resurrection through the use of thematic images from the Bible, such as Daniel in the lion's den and Jonah in the great fish. An early symbol for the resurrection was a wreath that encircled the Greek letters *chi rho*, the first two letters of "Christ"; this image symbolized the triumph of resurrection over death. The actual moment of resurrection (which is not described in the Gospels) is not depicted directly for another millennium, when Gothic and then Renaissance artists such as Dürer, Raphael, and Rubens begin to show Jesus stepping out of a Roman-style sarcophagus or hovering in the air above an open tomb.

The themes of the afterlife and resurrection appear regularly in poetry and literature as well. John Donne (1572–1631), writer, Anglican minister, and the most famous representative of the seventeenth-century metaphysical poets, composed "Death Be Not Proud" as a fierce challenge to the (perceived) finality of death:

Death be not proud, though some have called thee
Mighty and dreadful, for, thou art not so,
For, those, whom thou think'st, thou dost overthrow,

Die not, poore death, nor yet canst thou kill me.
From rest and sleepe, which but thy pictures bee,
Much pleasure, then from thee, much more must flow,
And soonest our best men with thee doe goe,
Rest of their bones, and souls deliverie.
Thou art slave to Fate, Chance, kings, and desperate men,
And dost with poyson, warre, and sicknesse dwell,
And poppie, or charmes can make us sleepe as well,
And better then thy stroake; why swell'st thou then;
One short sleepe past, wee wake eternally,
And Death shall be no more, death thou shalt die!

This poem, like many of the works Donne wrote toward the end of his life, confronts death (in the first person) and tries to allay the fear that it inspires in many of us. For Donne, death is not so "mighty and dreadful," since death is not the end of life: those who die will live on eternally in heaven. In this way, the afterlife promises the *death* of death; once our souls awaken from their "short sleepe," then "Death shall be no more, death thou shalt die!" Donne offers an impassioned, confident belief in the world-to-come, but he does not give a specific description of what eternity entails.

Paradiso offers a stark and vivid contrast. In this third and final book of the *Divine Comedy*, Dante Alighieri provides a highly specific description of heaven and the world-to-come. Guided by Beatrice, his beloved muse, Dante travels through the nine celestial spheres of heaven. Every sphere represents a different abode for the reborn souls of the deceased, each one reflective of the behavior and character of human beings. When, at long last, Dante encounters the ninth heavenly sphere—the only one that contains angels within its borders—he gets intoxicated by the vision of an angelic assembly singing a song of praise to God:

What I saw seemed a smile of the universe;
thus my intoxication came in through hearing
and through sight.
Oh joy! Oh ineffable happiness! Oh life made

whole with love and peace! Oh riches secure
without greed! (27.4–9)

Dante bears witness to the joy of the heavenly host, an experience that
is marked by love and peace. In his ecstatic joy and "ineffable happiness,"
Dante feels that life has been made whole and complete. But he has not
yet reached the end of his journey—or of his vision. Dante's final sight
is that of the Empyrean, the highest heaven. The Empyrean, a medieval
name for the firmament and the dwelling place of God, consists of celestial beings so divine that they are made of pure light. It appears to Dante
in the form of a "white rose" surrounded by heavenly creatures that fly
about in circles

    like a swarm of bees that enflower themselves
at one moment and in the next return
where their labor ensavors itself,
    was descending into the great flower that is
adorned with so many petals and was rising thence
back up to where its love always spends its day.
    They all had faces of lively flame, wings of
gold, and the rest so white that no snow
reaches that limit. (31.7–15)

Emanating divine love, the celestial rose animates the beings who
"swarm" around it. The heavenly creatures are made of the light of pure
spirit, and the sight is blinding and unforgettable—the French illustrator
Gustave Doré (1832–83) famously captures the image of the celestial rose
in one of his illustrations of Dante's work. The poet longs for the light of
the world-to-come to turn toward our world:

    This secure and joyous kingdom, abounding
in people ancient and new, directed all its sight
and love toward one mark.
    O triple light, that in a single star, flashing in

their sight, fulfill them so, gaze down here at our
tempest! (31.25–30)

In addition to the angels, the kingdom of God—heaven and the afterlife—is made up of the reborn souls of men and women, both old and
new, who have died throughout the ages. Life in the world-to-come is
purely spiritual in nature. It revolves around, and is nourished by, a divine
center that anchors and elevates it. A glimpse of this world allows Dante
to return to his own world a wiser, more enlightened person.

As we have seen, the idea of rebirth is often conveyed in the religious context through the image of a valley. This sometimes occurs in the literary
context as well. In Steinbeck's novel *East of Eden* (which I first referenced
in chapter 3), the Salinas Valley in Northern California plays a central role
in the story. While the valley provides the setting for several of Steinbeck's
works, it is most prominent in *East of Eden*. Steinbeck's working title for
the novel was, in fact, "The Salinas Valley," and he has described his fic-
tional tale as "a sort of autobiography of the Salinas Valley."

The narrator opens *East of Eden* with a lyrical reminiscence of the valley, recounting the sights, smells, and other memories of his childhood:

> The Salinas Valley is in Northern California. It is a long narrow swale
> between two ranges of mountains, and the Salinas River winds and
> twists up the center until it falls at last into Monterey Bay.
>
> I remember my childhood names for grasses and secret flowers.
> I remember where a toad may live and what time the birds awaken
> in the summer—and what trees and seasons smelled like—how
> people looked and walked and smelled even. The memory of odors
> is very rich.

Following this evocative description of the valley, the narrator turns his
attention to the peaks, the eastern and western mountains that enclose
the lowlands and seem to embody the moral polarity of the Salinas region
as a whole:

I remember that the Gabilan Mountains to the east of the valley were light gay mountains full of sun and loveliness and a kind of invitation, so that you wanted to climb into their warm foothills almost as you want to climb into the lap of a beloved mother. They were beckoning mountains with a brown grass love. The Santa Lucias stood up against the sky to the west and kept the valley from the open sea, and they were dark and brooding—unfriendly and dangerous. I always found in myself a dread of west and a love of east. Where I ever got such an idea I cannot say, unless it could be that the morning came over the peaks of the Gabilans and the night drifted back from the ridges of the Santa Lucias. It may be that the birth and death of the day had some part in my feeling about the two ranges of mountains.

Through his symbolism, Steinbeck transforms the Salinas Valley into a stage that showcases the human struggle between good and evil, light and darkness, life and death. Some critics argue that the lush valley represents the lands where Adam and Eve dwell after they have been banished from Eden—it is a place filled with temptations. The mountains, critics claim, represent the ever-present tension between good and evil, geologic reflections of the human drama that unfolds beneath them.

Steinbeck, in my view, is far more subtle in his symbolism. The valley and peaks do not symbolize unfettered fertility or stark representations of good and evil, but the dynamic interplay between the forces of life, death, and rebirth:

I have spoken of the rich years when the rainfall was plentiful. But there were dry years too, and they put a terror on the valley. The water came in a thirty-year cycle. There would be five or six wet and wonderful years when there might be nineteen to twenty-five inches of rain, and the land would shout with grass. Then would come six or seven pretty good years of twelve to sixteen inches of rain. And then the dry years would come, and sometimes there would be only seven or eight inches of rain. The land dried up and the grasses headed out miserably a few inches high and great bare scabby places appeared in the valley. The live oaks got a crusty look and the sagebrush was

gray. The land cracked and the springs dried up and the cattle list-
lessly nibbled dry twigs. Then the farmers and the ranchers would be
filled with disgust for the Salinas Valley. The cows would grow thin
and sometimes starve to death. People would have to haul water in
barrels to their farms just for drinking. Some families would sell out
for nearly nothing and move away. And it never failed that during the
dry years the people forgot about the rich years, and during the wet
years they lost all memory of the dry years. It was always that way.

As primary a role as the Salinas Valley plays in *East of Eden*, it is the
human characters who dramatize the struggle between good and evil,
life and death. This is especially the case with regard to the father-son
relationships of Adam Trask and his sons, Aron and Caleb. Cal (short
for Caleb) in particular highlights the tension between the soul's desire
to be good and the pull of temptation. While one of the core ideas in
East of Eden is that sin and wickedness are innate and at times irresistible
human problems, the novel also offers the hope that every human being
possesses the capacity to transcend his or her darker impulses through
the exercise of free choice.

Steinbeck discusses freedom of choice through the narrative of Lee,
Adam's Chinese housekeeper. Lee informs Adam that, out of deep curiosity, he has researched the Hebrew word *timshel*, a word that appears in the
book of Genesis. The word is uttered during the story of Cain and Abel,
when God tells Cain that he has the freedom to choose whether or not
to overcome sin. It translates as "thou mayest." Lee believes that free will
is the key to human life, and that *timshel* might be the "most important
word in the world." The housekeeper recounts the results of his research:

This was the gold from our mining: "Thou mayest." The American
Standard translation orders men to triumph over sin (and you can
call sin ignorance). The King James translation makes a promise in
"Thou shalt," meaning that men will surely triumph over sin. But
the Hebrew word timshel—"Thou mayest"—that gives a choice.
For if "Thou mayest"—it is also true that "Thou mayest not." That
makes a man great and that gives him stature with the gods, for in his

weakness and his filth and his murder of his brother he has still the great choice. He can choose his course and fight it through and win.

Through the word *timshel*, Lee observes, God instructs Cain that his own free choice will determine whether he might conquer the temptation of sin (and its deadening effects on his soul) or, instead, succumb to it. Regardless of the depth of the sin, free will promises that there will always be a chance for redemption. With the valley as their stage, all of the main characters in *East of Eden* wrestle with moral dilemmas, and all of them face difficult choices. Despite wrongful actions that drag Cal into depravity and darkness, he receives a second chance from his father. At the end of his life (and the end of the novel), Adam gives Cal his blessing, though he does it indirectly:

> Adam looked up with sick weariness. His lips parted and failed and tried again. Then his lungs filled. He expelled the air and his lips combed the rushing sigh. His whispered word seemed to hang in the air: "Timshel!" His eyes closed and he slept.

Adam's last word is not only an expression of forgiveness, but the key to Cal's liberation. Cal now realizes that he himself holds the power to surmount his family's legacy of evil and death: he can begin again; he can be reborn. Cal struggles throughout the novel to find a middle ground between the poles of good and evil. While the biblical Cain is banished for his sin, Cal experiences forgiveness and redemption through *timshel*, his father's one-word blessing. With this newfound knowledge that he has the ability to control his own destiny, that he is not doomed to darkness, Cal can go forth into a new life (with Abra, his love interest). His life in the valley may be a journey of descent—his *yeridah*—but it is a journey that ultimately transforms him. *East of Eden* ends on a note of optimism, of belief that rebirth is possible not just for Cal, but for all of us.

The idea that we can be reborn after an experience of "death" is a compelling one, and it is an idea that is not limited to religious thinkers and mystics. While our souls cannot live on eternally until after we have shuffled off our mortal coil, we *can* experience forgiveness, second chances, and life-altering transformations in the here and now. Perhaps those human events, as analogies of sorts, are our best hope for gaining a taste of what "heaven" might be like. If rebirth and resurrection are possible in this world, why is it far-fetched to imagine they will be possible in the world-to-come?

Human existence is a series of valleys and peaks, descents and ascents. When all seems lost, we sometimes find new opportunities and new possibilities: jobs, relationships, experiences, love. Sometimes, all we can muster when we are in the dark and frightening places is the will to go on. My own experience of driving from Chicago to the Shenandoah Valley helped to pull me out of a state of despair and self-pity; it allowed me to accept uncertainty as the price I'd need to pay to enter the next chapter of my life, whatever that might be. For reasons I still don't understand, the valley gave me strength and resolve. Maybe it was the contrast between my inner state and the outer beauty of the mountains around me.

At times, the will simply to go on may be enough. In light of the limits of our human capacities, perhaps will is all we have—and all we need to have. The Zionist leader Theodore Herzl (1860–1904) famously wrote of the Jewish state, his promised land, "If you will it, it is no dream." When it comes to the afterlife, perhaps we ought to claim similarly, "If you will it, it is no illusion." Either our aspiration will turn out to be a lie, or it will guide and ground our lives, give us a sense of purpose and meaning, and elevate us with the strength and courage to persevere. We can't know which is the truth, not yet and not while we are still on this earth. But we will all know soon enough.

We are all walking through the valley of shadows. Yet our tradition teaches that there is more to come, that abundance and love await us at the end of our journeys.

Conclusion

MOST SPIRITUALITY BOOKS CLAIM TO provide quick and clear paths to personal growth, and they provide step-by-step programs that purport to show readers how to achieve all their goals and fulfill all their dreams. I offer a different, and I think more honest, approach. While the ultimate message of this book is one of comfort and hope, I give no neat and clean set of answers to life's questions and challenges. *Eight Questions of Faith* is more of a traveler's guide than a rule book, a project that brings together texts and voices from the past and present in an effort to help us find meaning and purpose on the human journey. That goal is ambitious enough, and the task has been humbling.

It is a goal that also seems appropriate to life as I have experienced and tried to make sense of it, especially in recent years.

In the end, this book became as much a meditation on midlife as it is an exploration of eight key questions from the Bible. The questions that I have discussed in these pages have helped me to face and work through several important life transitions, and they have taught me a number of invaluable life lessons. As I have strived to fathom and surmount my existential challenges, those same questions have shown me that I am not alone in my struggles. The search for wisdom is universal and lifelong, and it is daunting. Still, I cannot imagine a more worthy, even noble, pursuit.

One of the great lessons I have learned is that I am just like everybody else. My youthful fantasies about becoming a superman, about perfecting my mind, soul, and body, have been deconstructed by age and maturity. Whatever pretense I used to have about my own exceptionalism has been left by the side of the road; my self-absorption and narcissism, so present and damaging in my twenties and thirties, have been punctured by the collective realities of the human condition. I now belong to a community of seekers, searchers, and strugglers—I am part of the whole—and I share the same pain and perplexity, and experience the same trials and triumphs, as my fellow travelers.

I feel relieved. And less isolated. Still, there are times when I feel like an outlier, someone who lives at the edge of the camp. On a certain level, my sense of solitariness remains. As a childless bachelor pushing fifty, I wonder if I have made the right choices, if my priorities have always been appropriate, if, in my pursuit of unfettered freedom and unbridled self-expression, I have condemned myself to a life of loneliness and marginality.

Whatever my perception, I know that life is with people.

The queries in this book represent a kind of existential catchall for several important milestones in the human adventure. While, at times, I have used the questions as springboards for more general explorations of concepts such as mortality, responsibility, purpose, forbidden knowledge, and rebirth, I have tried to follow a specific trajectory. The book begins with a meditation on finitude and it ends with an examination of the afterlife. In between, the chapters follow what, I think, is a familiar catalog of human experiences and challenges, even though not all of us encounter them in a particular chronology. Yet who hasn't been afraid or felt abandoned? Who among us hasn't fallen short of their ideals, or strived to return to a place of wholeness?

I feel a gnawing sense of urgency about these questions, an urgency that is new for me. At their core, all of the questions in the book relate to matters of life and death. And for me, mortality is no longer theoretical, something I speculated about intellectually when I was younger. It is real, and it has hit home. My life is, at best, half over. What will I do with the time I have left? How much time *do* I have left? Will I play a role in addressing important existential issues?

Through this book, I have tried to address a number of these issues, and each chapter has represented my attempt to offer insights into the human condition.

I make the following claims:

~ We must go on with our lives, even in the face of uncertainty, struggle, despair, and suffering. Life may not be a given, but it is a gift.

~ Humility clarifies our self-perception. It instills in us the courage to accept our limitations and then become stronger human beings.

~ We must be responsible for one another, though the source of that moral authority, and of evil, is opaque.

~ The "fear" of God opens us to the true purpose of life—the experience of godliness within it.

~ The pursuit of knowledge should not be an end in itself. Some types of knowledge are too dangerous to possess.

~ Our misdeeds can separate us from God. Yet our awareness of that separation can catalyze healing and create a renewed relationship.

~ We all feel lost at different points in our lives, but a journey through the wilderness can lead to growth and transformation.

~ While we cannot know the nature of the world to come, we can experience the phenomena of death and rebirth in the here and now.

Each of the biblical questions highlighted in the chapters (and the concepts that it brings to the surface) is as relevant and pressing now as it was in ancient times—not just for me, but, when we are able and willing to ask it, for every one of us. The Bible may be the most famous book ever written, but it is held as sacred only by members of the three Abrahamic faith traditions. The questions and themes that Scripture raises, however, are universal in their reach and paramount in their import. Whether they are direct, suggestive, rhetorical, or pedagogic, these inquiries are provocative and sometimes painful. And they are indispensable to all of us.

Are we ready to voice the questions, or to hear them, ourselves? That depends on where we are in our lives. In my own self-assessment, it has taken me many years to ask—in an authentic, honest, and heartfelt way—the questions in this book. Until I reached the middle of my life's journey, most of them were purely academic; now, they burn inside me like coals, they influence my decisions, they direct my steps.

I am no longer interested in the pursuit of knowledge and wisdom for their own sakes. I am interested in my character. The Kotsker Rebbe writes that "the purpose of study is not to be a scholar, but to be a good man." I would argue that the purpose of *inquiry* is the same. I ask questions not to become smarter, but to be better.

As I wrote in the introduction, it is in the heart of unknowing, where the absence of clarity drives our yearning for answers, that we mature, evolve, and ultimately discover our correct path. That has certainly been my own experience so far. My confusion and uncertainty about what I have done, who I am, and where I am going have been discomforting and difficult, but they have fueled an intellectual curiosity and a spiritual need that have allowed me to grow and move forward as a man and a rabbi.

Perhaps more than anything, these past few years have taught me that nothing is perfect—no job, no relationship, no human life. They have also taught me that nothing is certain. So: *How do we learn to embrace imperfection and ambiguity?*

With this book, I hope to help others answer that question in their own way. In the process, I hope to improve my character and better cope with life's challenges. If I succeed, and if others can relate to or learn from my struggles, this was a worthy effort.

Acknowledgments

WHILE THIS IS MY TENTH book, it never ceases to amaze me how many people are often involved in the publication process. I am grateful to many for their help and support, but I want to single out several for special mention. First, I owe particular gratitude to Rabbi Barry Schwartz, director of the Jewish Publication Society (JPS). Barry contacted me about writing a book based on questions from the Bible soon after he read an essay I'd published in the *Forward* about my midlife journey. Little did he know that I'd already written a (rough) proposal on the same subject. I am indebted to Barry for his vision, encouragement, and leadership role throughout this book's development.

I am thankful to my literary agent, Linda Loewenthal, for shepherding the book through the early stages of the publishing process, and to Carol Hupping, managing editor of JPS, for playing such a vital editorial role in the book's later stages. David Van Biema and Carolyn and Frank Gill offered me valuable feedback and suggestions as well, in different ways and in other contexts.

I appreciate the encouragement and exposure provided to me by Benjamin Barer and Rabbi Or Rose at ON Torah, Alyssa Spatola at the *Huffington Post*, and Karen Meberg at Odyssey Networks. Together, they gave me wonderful platforms to test out some of the book's content prior to its publication. Many thanks to Dr. Melissa Browning for making the initial introductions. I also thank my colleague and friend Kristi Dale at Patheos for her unwavering enthusiasm.

Finally, John Fairfield, Ed Martin, and Trina Trotter Nussbaum at the Center for Interfaith Engagement helped me carve out the time and maintain the focus to finish the manuscript while I lived and worked in Virginia as a visiting Jewish scholar at Eastern Mennonite University. John, especially, was a constant sounding board and source of moral and spiritual support during those frigid winter months, and I now consider him a good friend. I will never forget my experience in the Shenandoah Valley.

OTHER WORKS BY NILES ELLIOT GOLDSTEIN

The Challenge of the Soul: A Guide for the Spiritual Warrior
(Random House, 2009)

Craving the Divine: A Spiritual Guide for Today's Perplexed
(Paulist Press, 2007)

Gonzo Judaism: A Bold Path for Renewing an Ancient Faith
(St. Martin's Press, 2006)

Lost Souls: Finding Hope in the Heart of Darkness
(Random House, 2002)

*God at the Edge: Searching for the Divine in Uncomfortable and
Unexpected Places* (Random House, 2000)

Duties of the Soul: The Role of Commandments in Liberal Judaism
(UAHC Press, 1998)

*Spiritual Manifestos: Visions for Renewed Religious Life in America
from Young Spiritual Leaders of Many Faiths*
(Jewish Lights, 1998)

Forests of the Night: The Fear of God in Early Hasidic Thought
(Jason Aronson, 1996)

Judaism and Spiritual Ethics (UAHC Press, 1996)

CPSIA information can be obtained
at www.ICGtesting.com
Printed in the USA
LVHW020956061220
673435LV00006B/459